ENHANCING
TRUST

THE ECFA STORY

ISBN: 978-1-936233-23-6

Table of Contents

Appreciation

ECFA started as an experiment and grew into a powerful force enhancing trust for Christ-centered churches and ministries—all dedicated to advancing God's Kingdom. Its history is braided with the story of the evangelical world, Christ-centered churches and other organizations, and the donors who support them.

ECFA is a testimony to the power of volunteerism. It was the first all voluntary nonprofit industry group established solely for the purpose of promoting financial accountability. ECFA would never have achieved its significant status inside and outside the evangelical community without the dedication and commitment of the ECFA board of directors, committee members, and other volunteers, plus the support of its members. You may easily recognize the names of some of the early ECFA pioneers; the names of others are more obscure. All served very important roles.

During the early years and at key points throughout ECFA's history, individuals, foundations, and member organizations stepped up to provide needed financial support to keep ECFA strong.

The compilation of this history was only possible because of the interest and support of Mark Holbrook, who served as ECFA's board chair from 2010 to 2013. He was concerned that the wealth of ECFA's history, especially related to the founding years, should be preserved as an increasing number of ECFA's initial leaders were promoted to their heavenly home.

Mark generously provided the research assistance of Garnette Black to initially facilitate this project. She conducted personal interviews with ECFA presidents Olan Hendrix, Art Borden, Paul Nelson, and Dan Busby. In addition to former staff members, former board members were also interviewed: Joel Aarsvold, Richard Capin, Steve Douglass, Jerry Bridges, Jack Frizen, John Pearson, Mark Holbrook, Sylvia Nash, Gordon Loux, Rollin Van Broekhoven, Tom McCabe, Chip Grange, and Michael Batts. After transcribing voluminous notes, Garnette wrote an initial narrative that served as the basis for further writing and the eventual publishing of this book.

Information was also provided by James Canning, one of the original Standards Committee members, who researched and documented ECFA's impact in his doctoral dissertation titled "Financial Accountability in Non-Profit Organizations: The Impact of the Evangelical Council for Financial Accountability" (Claremont Graduate University, 2002).

ECFA's staff also provided valued assistance on this project. They include Joy May, who provided layout and publishing assistance; Travis Huntsman, who designed the book cover; and Michael Martin, who assisted with the final writing and editing of this book.

Today ECFA stands on the shoulders of an army of more than 2,000 members, volunteers, funders, and staff. They are the heroes and heroines of the ECFA story!

Introduction

ECFA's history reminds us
—and future generations—
of God's faithfulness.

After 40 years of wandering in the wilderness, the Israelites entered the Promised Land. Just as it took a miracle to get them out of Egypt, it took just as big of a miracle to get them into Canaan. Just as God parted the Red Sea for Moses, He parted the Jordan River for Joshua. Both miracles happened so that each generation would know the Lord was with them in their time of need.

In Joshua 3 and 4, we learn that the Jordan River was at flood stage, which meant it was far too deep and far too swift for several million Jews and their livestock to safely cross over. So, Joshua told the priests to lift the Ark of the Covenant on their shoulders and step out into the water. The moment their feet touched the swirling muddy water, the river stopped flowing and the ground beneath their feet dried up. The priests and the Ark remained in the riverbed while the people hurried across. The men of Reuben, Gad, and the half-tribe of Manasseh, crossed over the Jordan armed and in front of the Israelites as Moses directed them.

It was a mighty miracle of God—a moment to be remembered forever. But Joshua knew that *even mighty miracles could be forgotten unless we do something to remember them.* So he instructed 12 men—one from each tribe—to take a large stone from the middle of the riverbed where the priests were standing with the Ark of the Covenant. Each man was to take the stone, put it on his shoulder, and carry it to the place where the Israelites would camp that night—a place called Gilgal. As soon as the men had carried the stones from the Jordan River, the priests followed them. The moment the priests stepped on the west bank, the water started flowing again.

When the men got to Gilgal, Joshua had them build a monument—a memorial—from those 12 stones where the priest had stood with the Ark. He had two things in mind: First, it was a teaching tool for future generations. Joshua knew that the younger generation would look at that pile of stones and say, "What's this all about?" And their fathers would say, "Those stones came from the Jordan River on the day God performed a miracle so our people could walk across on dry ground."

Second, it was a testimony to the watching world. Joshua 4:24 says, "He did this so that all the peoples of the earth might know that the hand of the LORD is powerful." Those 12 stones reminded the nation of what God had done. They were visual evidence that in the moment of crisis, God had brought His people safely across the Jordan River. They testified to God's faithfulness in the past so that future generations would know that they too could trust the Lord. When the pagans saw those stones, they would know that the God of Israel was a mighty God.

Memorials remind us—and future generations—of what God has done. At this point in ECFA's history, it is appropriate to document God's faithfulness through the years. It is a way of placing stones so we will never forget what God has done.

In the mid-1970s, a number of charity fundraising abuses were being reported in the press, and the public was becoming increasingly concerned. The charities had not broken any federal laws, for there were virtually no laws regulating charities at that time. And the state and local laws that did exist were mostly ineffectual, unenforceable, unenforced, or haphazardly administered.[1]

The fundraising abuses caught the attention of Congress, and onerous legislation was introduced. As a result, the need for an accreditation organization in the evangelical world—an ECFA—began to be more apparent, and the adoption of a set of pass-fail standards launched peer-based self-regulation for Christ-centered organizations. A great movement was on its way, like the morning's first draft of sunlight. It started at a meeting of Christian leaders in Chicago in 1977, but it didn't end there.

As Jim Canning explains in his doctoral dissertation describing ECFA's formative years,

> When [ECFA] was established in 1979, few organizations met all of ECFA's standards. Most had to make some changes in their practices in order to meet the requirements for membership. Because many organizations were not audited at the time, obtaining auditors and undergoing an annual audit was a frequent area requiring change. In addition, many organizations had to increase the size of their boards with additional volunteers or decrease the number of employees holding board membership. . . . Prior to 1979, few organizations voluntarily provided financial information to the public, so this represented a radical

change for most organizations. In general, more significant changes were required for small and mid-sized organizations than for large ones.[2]

While ECFA's initial focus was on transparency and the proper use of charitable resources, it was not long until it became apparent that it was also important to emphasize excellence in governance and fundraising/stewardship as well.

ECFA's mission is simple: "Enhancing trust in Christ-centered churches and ministries." By adhering to ECFA's Seven Standards of Responsible Stewardship™, accredited organizations may display ECFA's respected seal, communicating to donors and the giving public that they are worthy of trust and support.

It is hard to imagine where evangelical organizations would be today without ECFA—if those early ministry leaders had not united in the late 1970s in the wake of financial and moral scandals rocking the religious nonprofit community. Lauren Libby, former ECFA board member and president of Trans World Radio, remarked, "If ECFA had not been formed, another organization would have been needed to fill its role."

By forming ECFA, these leaders chose to demonstrate integrity within the body of Christ to an increasingly skeptical world watching for the first sign of impropriety.

ECFA's story is an exciting testimony to God's faithfulness and provision. As we anticipate ECFA's future, let this book serve as a memorial for all He has done.

Dan Busby, ECFA President (2008–Present)

Chapter One

Before There Was an ECFA

"When you're publicly accountable, people feel more comfortable about you. They won't tend to accuse you of hiding funds or doing other things wrong financially."

Stephen Douglass, President, Cru

In the Great Commission, Christ urged His followers to share the good news of salvation with a lost and hurting world (Matthew 28:19–20). The history of ECFA—and the Christian church as a whole—can be traced back to these final words that Jesus Christ shared on earth with His disciples.

The term "evangelical" originates from the Greek, meaning "the good news" or the "gospel."[1] From its inception, ECFA has always been thoroughly evangelical. The first word of the organization's very name—Evangelical Council for Financial Accountability—evidences its commitment to evangelicalism.

The first standard required of ECFA members is that they "shall subscribe to a written statement of faith clearly affirming a commitment to the evangelical Christian faith, or shall otherwise demonstrate such commitment, and shall operate in accordance with biblical truths and practices" (Appendix 1). Commitment to the evangelical faith is the fundamental element that holds ECFA's members together.

Evangelicalism in the United States

Evangelicalism has been alive and well in the United States since the founding of our country. For example, the Mayflower Compact of 1620—one of the oldest governing documents in American history—explicitly states that the early settlers were establishing the colony for the glory of God and advancement of the Christian faith.

Congregations assembled and churches were built in America dating back to the 17th century. In the early 1800s, evangelical church denominations began to develop. The volunteer societies (from political parties to musical societies) that arose in the late 1700s and the early 1800s were a precursor to today's parachurch organizations.

Missionary-sending organizations related to the newly-formed denominations began springing up in the 1880s. Around the same time, the "faith missions" movement also began. These groups were uncompromisingly evangelical, but interdenominational. Concurrent with the establishment of missionary organizations were rescue missions, some of the earliest parachurch ministries.

The 1900s saw an explosion of evangelical churches, denominations, parachurch organizations, and institutions of higher education in the United States. Many of these new organizations were formed in the early part of the century, but with the end of World War II, the United States witnessed a quiet tsunami of hundreds of new ministries. Members of the military returning home brought with them gratitude, awareness, and a God-given passion to make a difference in the world. They wanted to minister across a wide spectrum of needs, such as prison outreaches, hunger relief, and evangelism.

These visionary leaders had the passion, but often they did not have advanced education or professional training to manage their blossoming organizations. It was common to operate out of a checkbook and not compile formal accounting records.

Growth and development of the nonprofit sector

As a country founded on the principle of limited government, private associations have always played a major role in meeting many of the most important needs of American society.

This was noted by French historian and politician Alexis de Tocqueville, who, upon visiting the United States in the 1830s, captured this unique aspect of American culture in writing:

> Americans of all ages, all conditions, and all disposi-
> tions constantly form associations. They have not
> only commercial and manufacturing companies, in
> which all take part, but associations of a thousand
> other kinds, religious, moral, serious, futile, general
> or restricted, enormous or diminutive. The Americans
> make associations to give entertainments, to found
> seminaries, to build inns, to construct churches, to
> diffuse books, to send missionaries to the antibodies;

in this manner they found hospitals, prisons, and schools. If it is proposed to inculcate some truth or foster some feeling by the encouragement of a great example, they form a society. Wherever at the head of some new undertaking you see the government in France, or a man of a rank in England, in the United States you will be sure to find an association.[2]

As part of this culture of relying on voluntary associations, Christian churches and parachurch organizations developed alongside other religious and secular charities to become what is known today as the nonprofit sector.

Federal tax exemption for American nonprofit organizations dates back to the early 1900s. When Congress passed the Revenue Act of 1913, the basis of our current federal income tax system, it exempted "any corporation or association organized and operated exclusively for religious, charitable, scientific, or educational purposes" in part out of recognition for the vital benefits that these organizations provide to society. Four years later in the War Revenue Act of 1917, Congress took another major step forward in providing the charitable contribution tax deduction for individuals as a way to incentivize giving and grow the nonprofit sector.

These two incentives for nonprofits have remained an important feature of the tax code ever since, despite being challenged politically from time to time, and have significantly contributed to the nonprofit sector's dramatic growth through the years. By one estimate, there were 12,500 charitable tax-exempt organizations registered with the IRS in 1940, along with approximately 180,000 non-registered religious congregations. Between 1940 and 1980, the number of charitable tax-exempt organizations increased dramatically to approximately 320,000 in addition to 336,000 religious congregations. By 2013, the number of charities exploded to around one million, while the number of congregations was estimated at 345,000.[3]

More accountability expected from nonprofits

With the growth in size and scope of the nonprofit sector, government leaders began sensing a need for greater oversight of religious and other charitable organizations. This was largely in response to fears that favorable tax treatment for charities was being abused for private benefit.

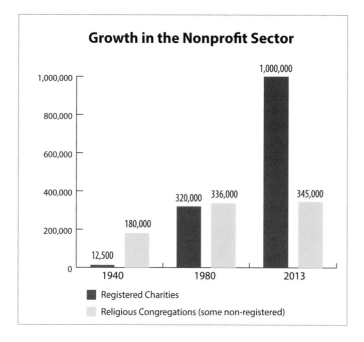

For many years, the government was limited in regulating charitable activities. The IRS introduced the Form 990 annual information return in the 1940s as a reporting requirement for most public charities. There was, and still is, an exemption for churches and church-related organizations. By 1976, the Form 990 was only a modest two pages with three and one-half pages of instructions.[4] Additionally, it was very difficult for the general public to access this information because until the late 1980s an interested person had to request a copy of the Form 990 directly from the IRS—a rather slow and burdensome method of public disclosure.

In the late 1970s, few nonprofit organizations had an annual audit or published financial statements. During this era, while nonprofits often publicly disclosed program results, the number of volunteers, and other related figures, it was uncommon for a nonprofit organization to openly share financial data. It was not unusual for religious organizations to take the position that they were only accountable to God.

A related issue at the time was the general lack of accounting standards for nonprofit organizations. Not until the late 1970s did the Financial Accounting Standards Board (FASB) even begin to consider the development of a specific set of accounting principles for nonprofit organizations. There were a series of industry audit guides for nonprofits that practitioners could rely upon, but they lacked the authority to constitute generally accepted accounting principles.

Steve Douglass, president of Cru (formerly Campus Crusade for Christ), was then vice president of administration for the ministry. He still vividly remembers visiting Bill Kanaga, the managing partner of Arthur Young and Company (now Ernst and Young). Steve asked Bill where things were going in the nonprofit world in terms of reporting on finances. Cru, along with almost all Christian ministries at that time, had the policy of releasing annual report information on a "need to know" basis.

Stephen Douglass

Bill explained that a strong trend was beginning which would soon demand of Christian ministries that they publish their annual reports and distribute them freely. Because of Bill Kanaga's counsel, Steve went back to Bill Bright, the founder and president of Cru, and strongly recommended that the ministry publish an annual report. Furthermore, he recommended that they hire a large, very visible Big Eight accounting firm rather than the smaller one they had been using. Bill Bright approved, and Arthur Young & Company started performing Cru's audit. The ministry soon produced its first widely published annual report.

That same year, the media specifically focused on financial disclosure. Reporters were going from ministry to ministry asking, "Where is your annual report? Do you even have one? What are you hiding?" One of these reporters came to Cru. Steve distinctly remembers sitting across the table from him. The reporter asked, "Well, I don't suppose you have an annual report, do you?" Steve slid it across the Formica tabletop into the hands of the reporter. The

interview terminated quickly; Cru was one of only three
nonprofits confronted by the reporter that did actually have
a publicly-available annual report.

Steve observed, "When you're publicly accountable, people
feel more comfortable about you. They won't tend to accuse
you of hiding funds or doing other things wrong, financially."[5]

Few organizations at that time took the initiative to increase
their accountability like Cru. In 1979 came what President
Jimmy Carter described in a televised speech to the nation as
a "crisis of confidence." He was referring to U.S. citizens' lack
of confidence in their government, but he might just as well
have been talking about the erosion of public confidence in
nonprofit organizations.

Congress and the press began expressing concern over what
they considered to be deceptive fundraising appeals, both in
secular and religious nonprofits. But in light of the First
Amendment, there was a question of how far the federal
government could go with respect to religious nonprofits.
Soon, several scandals in the nonprofit world would illustrate
the public's growing concerns over donating to charities.
These and others had the potential to destroy the good-faith
giving of many American donors.

In a January 6, 1980 essay published in Parade magazine,
author and charity researcher Carl Bakal chronicles these
incidents:

> [T]he Asthmatic Children's Foundation had raised
> some $10 million over a 10-year period for its stated

purpose of helping asthmatic children. However, a close examination of the foundation's records showed that only about 14 cents of every dollar collected went for this purpose. The rest was spent on fundraising and administrative costs.

In Washington, D.C., about the same time, a United Police Fund was launched "to aid the widows and orphans of slain policemen." With the aid of a tear-jerking mail appeal signed by a Congressman, the fund raised $140,121 in less than a year. Of this, the "widows and orphans" received only $18,000— only 13 percent of the sum raised. The rest went for "expenses, fees, and a salaried employee."

Where Do Charity Billions Go?

Public watchdogs are needed to monitor huge sums raised by telethons and other appeals

Parade, January 6, 1980

The widows and orphans were lucky. The Foundation for Research and Education in Sickle Cell Disease has charged that not one penny of the $218,000 reportedly raised on a New York telethon ever reached their organization.

. . .

An official of a large Eastern city once complained that any group could get a permit to collect money for "snowblind Eskimos and report that 99 percent of the money was used for administrative costs. There would be nothing we could do."[6]

Then there were the Pallottine Fathers, a Roman Catholic order, operating out of a Baltimore warehouse. It was a highly sophisticated, tightly secured multi-million dollar mail order fundraising operation. It was reported it spent less than three percent of the estimated $20 million it raised for its proclaimed purpose of helping the "starving sick or naked overseas." Much of the balance was invested in questionable real estate and other business deals or diverted by the order's fundraising director into secret bank accounts and squandered on fellow Pallottines, friends, and relatives.[7]

In a three-year span (November 1972–1975), the Pallottines sent out 270 million fundraising letters, including millions of Christmas cards, ballpoint pens, letter openers, and a mailing called "the Pallottine sweepstakes." In the sweepstakes, gifts such as cars and pool tables were given to the lucky winners, all in hopes of bringing in contributions for the order's overseas mission.[8]

All this led Rep. Charles H. Wilson (D-CA) to introduce H.R. 41, a charity disclosure bill, on January 4, 1977. It would generally require any group seeking gifts by mail, including religious organizations, to provide data on where the money would go and how much of it would be used for overhead. Several other more restrictive proposals were already being formulated by concerned lawmakers.

The legislation was supported by many secular charities, including the American Heart Association, the National Kidney Foundation, the American Lung Association, and the Save the Children Federation.

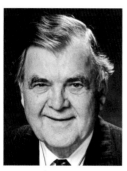

Ted Engstrom

With H.R. 41 still in play in the House, Senator Mark Hatfield (R-OR) met with Ted Engstrom, president of World Vision, and George Wilson, executive vice president of the Billy Graham Evangelistic Association, in Hatfield's office. (Senator Hatfield was a World Vision board member at this time, so he well understood the effect the legislation would have on Christ-centered ministries.) He challenged them to monitor evangelical nonprofit organizations with some form of a "Christian Better Business Bureau" or face the potential of government intervention.

George Wilson

While strong opposition by religious groups ultimately prevented passage of H.R. 41, out of this meeting emerged the concept of what would become ECFA.

Chapter Two

Peer Accountability Takes Hold

"Government intervention is too often
like a female elephant that saw an untended nest
of quail eggs beside the road.
The nest aroused her maternal instincts,
which she immediately expressed by
sitting on the eggs. Her motivation may have been
unquestionably pure, but there is no question
that the result was somewhat extreme!"

Stan Mooneyham, Past President,
World Vision International

Formative meetings of ECFA's visionaries

Things came to a head in late 1977. The challenge from
Senator Mark Hatfield left Ted Engstrom with the sure
knowledge that some action must be taken. He sent out the
call for a December 9 meeting. Representatives of more
than 30 ministries gathered in Chicago on a blustery winter

day to discuss their concerns. Among
the attendees were Ted Engstrom,
president of World Vision, and Stanley
Mooneyham, president of World
Vision International. These two were
selected as co-chairs for the group.

Stan, who eventually became an
honorary ECFA board member, recalled   Stan Mooneyham
the events in a speech he later gave at the
September 11, 1979, inaugural membership meeting in
Chicago.

> In the fall of 1977, just as I was about to ask a group of
> like-minded leaders to come together to consider a
> course of action, I learned that George Wilson [at the
> Billy Graham Evangelistic Association] was on the
> verge of doing the same thing with a group of people
> primarily involved in broadcasting. We decided to
> combine the two meetings and more than 30
> organizations were represented at the first gathering.
>
> At that meeting, Senator Hatfield told us through his
> assistant, Tom Getman, that "Legislation is not
> important; disclosure is. . . . A voluntary disclosure
> program can be developed that will preclude the
> necessity of federal intervention in the philanthropic
> and religious sector."
>
> . . .
>
> It was, without exaggeration, a historic day. Rarely
> had a group so diverse, all of whom cherished their

independence and freedom, agreed on a course of action that would be as far-reaching in its impact, as we did that day. Because the minority of irresponsible and fraudulent charity organizations reflect on the good name of us all, we, perhaps even more than a concerned public and an alert press, want to see high standards of ethics and financial accountability maintained by all organizations—especially ours—which appeal to the public for funds.

Ted, speaking at the same meeting as Chairman of the Temporary Board of Directors, gave the following address:

I would like us to turn our attention, for a few moments, to the "spiritual ministry" which the ECFA performs. If the phrase "spiritual ministry" sounds strange to you, let me explain.

I'm going to describe the ministry of ECFA by first turning our attention to the Apostle Paul's second letter to the Corinthian Church. Listen to some of the statements he makes regarding the integrity of his ministry with them:

(In Chapter One) "[O]ur activities in this world, particularly our dealings with you, have been absolutely above board and sincere before God."

(In Chapter Three and Four in the Phillips translation) "With this hope in our hearts (future glory) we are quite frank and open in

our ministry. . . . We use no hocus-pocus, no
clever tricks, no dishonest manipulation of the
Word of God. We speak the plain truth and so
commend ourselves to every man's conscience
in the sight of God."

Do you see what permeates Paul's ministry? Do you
catch the strength of his character?

In a day when speech was filled with double-meaning
and tongue-in-cheek statements, Paul was demonstra-
ting faultless integrity.

The Apostle Peter put it this way in his first letter
(chapter three—Phillips): "Make sure that your
conscience is perfectly clear, so that if men should
speak slanderously of you as rogues, they may come
to feel ashamed of themselves for libeling your good
Christian behavior."

Throughout their ministry, these early Christians
sought to exemplify the highest character and open,
frank and truthful conduct. What an example for us to
follow in our ministries!

Now the ECFA is committed to maintaining these
same standards of behavior among its members. Its
ministry is to uphold and encourage the integrity
and trustworthiness of evangelical organizations
ministering in the name of Jesus Christ.

. . .

I believe the ECFA provides a ministry to qualified evangelical organizations. . . . Two areas come to mind.

One is an increased ability for member organizations of ECFA to focus on their unique ministry without spending resources and time on repeatedly defending themselves before a critical public. They would be free to once again give their most creative energies to the task to which God has called them. We must keep ever before us the needs and hurts of a world lost without Christ, for this is inherent within the very name "Evangelical." Maintaining the ECFA seal of approval can greatly assist us in keeping our attention on service to the people and purposes which called our organizations into existence.

Second, I believe greater enthusiasm for giving to our various organizations will be generated. As confidence is built in organizations who practice voluntary financial disclosure, so too will funds increase. Evangelicals are a very generous people, motivated by the generosity of Christ Himself. If they can find trustworthy organizations in which to express their generosity, they will be more than willing to respond to appeals for assistance.

Ted Engstrom and George Wilson had great uneasiness about the direction that nonprofits were heading. In the face of so many scandals in the nonprofit sector, these were forward thinkers who knew it was time to clean up their side of the street. The impending option was to have the government intervene via regulations, laws, and changes to the tax code. The founders were also worried that the legislation being considered would place an intolerable and costly administrative burden on nonprofit organizations.

Moreover, as Christ-centered organizations, it was in their best interest to regulate themselves and to choose to do the right thing—for congregations, for staff and employees, for donors, and especially, as ambassadors of the Word.

Martin Luther King, Jr. once said, "Faith is taking the first step even when you don't see the whole staircase."[1] The first steps for ECFA, taken in faith, were these three unanimous actions at that first assembly:

1) To endorse and encourage voluntary public disclosure of finances by evangelical Christian organizations.

2) To create a committee that would establish uniform standards of financial disclosure for these organizations.

3) To instruct the committee to prepare a feasibility study on implementing the uniform standards through one or more certifying bodies.

Several of the large radio and television ministries voiced much opposition to the creation of a certifying overseer— some of whom later struggled with financial scandal. At the meetings, a bank of lawyers sat in the front row. They represented large organizations whose leaders led lavish lifestyles. They opposed the idea of full disclosure and did not want to give information to anyone who asked for it.

The first meeting of the Financial Disclosure Committee was held on June 12, 1978. The rationale for the meeting was unambiguously captured in the minutes:

> A meeting was called to draft guidelines for financial disclosure. This committee was called into being as an ad hoc group of Christian leaders who are concerned about a growing need for financial self-regulation by evangelical Christian organizations. This [larger] group, which met in Chicago on December 9, 1977, requested [chairs] Stan Mooneyham and George Wilson to establish a committee and report back on how the evangelical Christian community can exercise responsible self-discipline in financial disclosure.

The committee appointed by Stan Mooneyham and George Wilson selected Ted Engstrom as chairman and Eldon J. Howard as secretary.[2] The committee reviewed the existing financial and accounting standards for nonprofit organizations from the American Institute of Certified Public Accountants, Interdenominational Foreign Mission Association, Canadian Institute of Chartered Accountants, the ethics committee of the National Religious Broadcasters, and

Eldon J. Howard

the Better Business Bureau. At the conclusion of the meeting, the committee recommended two possible courses of action:

1) A consortium of Christian organizations that would establish a board made up of representatives from those

organizations. It would work in concert with government and public accounting bodies to establish proper financial disclosure for Christian organizations. The name suggested for this body was the Christian Organizations Financial Disclosure Consortium.

2) A separate accrediting body to accomplish the same objectives as the consortium.

On October 19, 1978, the Financial Disclosure Committee met for a second time in Chicago and decided to go with option number two. The Committee concluded that one umbrella organization was the desirable structure. This recommendation would be presented at an afternoon meeting to the larger group of prospective member organizations. At that presentation, the larger group was asked to develop articles of incorporation, bylaws, standards of conduct, and a budget for the first year of operation. The temporary working title for the organization was Association of Religious Nonprofit Organizations.

The committee met again, early the following year, on January 4 and 5, 1979. It reviewed those foundational documents and the name Evangelical Christian Financial Disclosure Bureau was proposed.

On March 1, 1979, the Financial Disclosure Committee met in the morning and presented its proposals to the group of prospective member organizations in the afternoon. Again, members of the larger group took action as they adopted the name Evangelical Council for Financial Accountability, adopted the articles of incorporation, adopted the bylaws with proposed amendments to be finalized by the temporary board of directors, and elected members to an initial board of directors.

The group was dedicated, committed, and gaining momentum.

First board and member meetings

On May 15, 1979, the first meeting of ECFA's board of directors was held, with Ted Engstrom presiding. Dr. Engstrom opened the meeting by sharing from 1 Corinthians 12–13. Then he had an announcement to make. ECFA had filed for incorporation in Minnesota, breathing life into ECFA as a new legal entity.

Next, the board discussed a physical location for offices. It determined that, for the first year, there should be a presence in Washington, D.C., perhaps sharing space with Prison Fellowship. Another option was to share space with the National Association of Evangelicals.

At this same meeting, George Wilson and Stan Mooneyham were named honorary members of that first board. As a final item, Jerry Bridges of The Navigators was tasked to form a Standards Committee that would develop an application for membership.

Jerry Bridges

ECFA was now firmly grounded as an organization. In July 1979, Ted Engstrom, chairman, sent a letter to 2,308 ministry leaders

announcing the very first member meeting for the Evangelical
Council for Financial Accountability to be held on September
11, at 1:00 p.m. at the O'Hare Marriott Hotel near the airport
in Chicago. In this letter, Ted Engstrom named George Wilson
and Stan Mooneyham as the prime movers for this enterprise.

The inaugural meeting of ECFA was held in Chicago as planned.
The participants drank ice water, not soft drinks. The hotel
wanted 75 cents per soda can—too much for an afternoon thirst
quencher. It was in this context of money consciousness that
ECFA moved forward.[3] With a few minor amendments, it
approved the Standards Committee's proposed application
requirements, the board unanimously
adopted a statement of faith, and approved
the seven standards of accountability to be
applied to accredited organizations.

Joel Aarsvold, of the Billy Graham
Evangelistic Association and the first
ECFA board secretary, remembers that
his biggest thrill was seeing the Lord
blend together many diverse organizations, all structured differently—some
just husband and wife with a few
outsiders on the board, some regional,
and some national.

Joel Aarsvold

Attorney Chip Grange, another member
of the initial Standards Committee, said:

> I appreciated that there was a
> spiritual center from the

Chip Grange

beginning, a genuine awareness among those involved that they were trying to do more than stop onerous legislation from being passed in Congress. I can still remember Ted Engstrom praying for wisdom and direction for the board and the Standards Committee.[4]

ECFA's time-tested approach to self-regulation

The die had been cast. Organizations would apply for accreditation voluntarily under a peer accountability concept. To be accredited, an organization would have to follow all of ECFA's standards, all of the time. Accredited organizations must be evangelical in faith, have an independent board, submit audited financial statements by independent certified public accountants, abide by the law, be appropriately transparent with their financial information, avoid conflicts of interest, and be truthful in their fundraising practices (see Appendix 2).

Chip Grange remembers how difficult it was to hammer out the first set of standards, which were approved at the inaugural meeting on September 11, 1979: "They didn't want them overly complex or too simple. By God's grace and through the collective wisdom of those early contributors, the first standards struck a credible balance. They had real teeth, were enforceable, but did not place unnecessary burdens on accredited ministries."[5]

The heart of ECFA's work—holding members in compliance with ECFA's standards—would generally be unheralded. This behind-closed-doors work, often involving ECFA's Standards

Committee, would be conducted consistently, confidentially, fairly, and under a redemptive approach. These concepts would only serve to enhance ECFA's credibility with each passing year.

It took approximately two years (1977–1979) to put together a charter, bylaws, statement of faith, and standards. The announcement of ECFA's formation in 1979 forestalled congressional action, but was met with considerable skepticism by the media, especially the Christian press. They felt ECFA would just give a slap on the hand to an offending organization.

They were wrong. A wave was welling up in the Christian world. Leaders recognized that even though the vast majority of organizations had nothing to hide, a future expectation of even greater transparency was beginning to crystallize. Just enough scandals had occurred to provide a springboard for action. They could all agree that they did not want the government imposing excessive regulation on nonprofit organizations.

The number of founding organizations accredited by ECFA reached nearly 150. It did not achieve optimistic forecasts of 1,000 or more members in its first few years; however, achieving this charter member level was a near-miraculous feat considering that ECFA required an independent financial audit of its members and relatively few nonprofits had audits at this time in history. The fledgling organization was moving forward against formidable odds.

Chapter Three

Blazing the Trail

"As the infant ECFA stepped up to face
the decade of the 1980s, only God could see the
gargantuan challenge PTL would present."

Dan Busby, ECFA President

By 1979, the infant organization had everything but a leader.
The visionaries realized that ECFA needed a strong leader
who knew the right people and would do the right things. Ted
Engstrom, who had met with Senator Mark Hatfield just after
HR-41 was introduced, was then president of World Vision.
Involved from the beginning, Ted knew that getting started
was not enough. Launching a self-regulating program for
nonprofits would be the tip of the iceberg.

What was needed beyond that was the buy-in of ministries.
Although many had been interested and supportive from the
beginning, continuing relationships would be what kept the
organization nourished.

At the time, Olan Hendrix was living in Pasadena, California, working nearly full-time at World Vision as director of leadership development under Ted Engstrom. They were very close. Ted came to Olan one afternoon and asked, "How about you taking over ECFA and get it running?" Olan answered, "Sure, I'd be glad to do that."

Olan Hendrix
Executive Director
(1979–1981)

Ted knew what he was doing in identifying Olan as a person qualified to lead ECFA. The fledgling organization needed someone who was respected in the world of Christ-centered nonprofits, someone who could approach them about accreditation with this new concept called ECFA—and Olan was ideally suited. He had been a consultant with many ministries and had personal relationships with their senior leaders. His experience suited him optimally to introduce this new organization.

Olan was invited to attend part of ECFA's first board meeting on May 15, 1979, as a candidate for executive director. He shared his vision with the board, and he answered questions from the directors. The board offered him the position with a modest annual salary. He would begin as soon as was practical. Although his salary came with no benefits and no staff, he was allowed the perk of working out of his home in Pasadena rather than in an office in Washington, D.C.

Olan's favorite way to describe ECFA to the press was "an idea whose time has come." Olan and the Standards Committee did all the work. He served as executive director from April

Los Angeles Times   Saturday, April 25, 1981 / Part I   **31**

Council Strives to Verify
Accountability of Fund Raisers

Seal of Approval Awarded to 162 Evangelical Units

JOSE GALVEZ / Los Angeles Times

Olan Hendrix, executive director of the ECFA, conducts business from his office in Pasadena.

Los Angeles Times (April 25, 1981) article highlights ECFA's progress.
Olan Hendrix is shown at his desk in the Pasadena, CA office.

1979 to October 1981, but he had never been interested in the position long-term. He knew the office needed to be in the Washington, D.C. area, and he wanted to remain in Pasadena. With ECFA successfully launched, Olan recommended Art Borden to succeed him. Olan highly respected Art for his years of service as a missionary, a church relations director for the American Bible Society, and a member of the executive committee of the National Association of Evangelicals.

Art took over the ECFA leadership reins in November 1981, when the organization was just two years old. Survival was far from assured, but Art was a trouble-shooter and a problem-solver. With a small staff and an annual budget of approximately $320,000, he dug in.

The Standards Committee, comprised of volunteers, was delegated tasks by ECFA's Board, including the formulation, interpretation, and enforcement of ECFA's Standards.

Art Borden
President (1981–1990)

An ECFA office was set up initially in Washington, D.C., and then moved to very modest quarters in Oakton, Virginia. It later moved to a somewhat larger headquarters in Herndon, and in 1990 to offices at Dulles Corner Park near Dulles Airport, where it stayed for nearly a decade. Art was experienced working on Capitol Hill. He helped ECFA become recognized with secular nonprofit organizations and foundations. In spite of its relatively small size, ECFA was gaining some identity outside the evangelical community.

ECFA's role on Capitol Hill

Under the leadership of Art Borden, ECFA began to develop formal interactions with Congress. On September 30, 1983, Art testified before the Senate Finance Committee's Sub-committee on Oversight of the Internal Revenue Service. The hearings were to provide testimony on legislation (S.1262, Church Audit Procedures Act of 1983) introduced by Senators Charles E. Grassley (R-IA), Jesse Helms (R-NC), and John East (R-NC) regarding heightened church audit procedures. The Subcommittee wanted to determine whether additional safeguards were necessary to preserve First Amendment freedoms for religious organizations.

The Church Audit Procedures Act (CAPA) was designed specifically to ensure that the IRS thought long and hard before auditing churches. It was also intended to ensure that examining a religious doctrine was not the basis for an audit. CAPA did not aim to shield churches, though, in the face of legitimate IRS inquiries related to church tax liability.

Art testified in favor of the legislation, stating that the bill would "assure that the IRS acts in accordance with the Constitution; and to introduce fairness into the procedures of the IRS." He continued, "This bill does not interfere with the IRS in carrying out its legally assigned responsibilities as an agency of the United States Government."[1]

The bill was enacted by Congress in 1984 and remains on the books today as Section 7611 of the Internal Revenue Code. It provides important protections for churches when faced with an IRS audit.

On October 6, 1987, Gordon Loux, ECFA board chair, and Chip Grange, ECFA board member, appeared before the Subcommittee on Oversight of the House Committee on Ways and Means chaired by Representative J. J. Pickle (D-TX). The focus of the hearing was on churches and other religious organizations, including television ministries, and their compliance with rules regarding private inurement, political activities, and lobbying. The subcommittee was seeking information with respect to the following questions: "How does the Internal Revenue Service interpret the law?"; "How does the IRS enforce the law?"; and "How do people and organizations comply with the law?"

Gordon testified, "Some are clamoring for the Government to become more involved in regulating Christian ministries. I do not believe that government intervention is the answer. . . . We believe in self-regulation because we feel it is more effective than Government regulation, and that it is more efficient."[2]

Equipping ministries for financial integrity

A comprehensive framework for accounting and reporting nonprofit finances was not conceived until the late 1970s, and even then, it took years before a single set of authoritative standards would take shape.

In the 1980s, more Christ-centered organizations began obtaining audits, which previously had been their primary obstacle to applying for ECFA accreditation. Before joining ECFA, many ministries utilized a cash or a modified accrual basis of accounting.[3] To obtain ECFA accreditation, these organizations had to raise the bar by changing their accounting method to the full accrual basis.

In December 1978, the American Institute of Certified Public Accountants (AICPA) issued *Accounting Principles and Reporting Practices for Certain Nonprofit Organizations* (78-10). This Statement of Position (SOP) was issued to recommend financial accounting principles not covered by other AICPA guides that related to specific types of nonprofit organizations:

Hospital Audit Guide (1972), Audits of Colleges and Universities (1973), Audits of Voluntary Health and Welfare Organizations (1974), and Audits of State and Local Governmental Units (1974).

The Financial Accounting Standards Board (FASB) released a research project by Robert N. Anthony: *Financial Accounting in Nonbusiness Organizations* in 1978. This was followed by *Statement of Financial Accounting Concepts No. 4, Objectives of Financial Reporting by Nonbusiness Organizations* in December 1980.

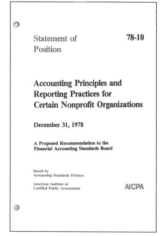

Statement of Position 78-10

While SOPs were not enforceable standards, they represented at the least majority positions of the AICPA's technical body and were designed to influence FASB and other authoritative rule-makers in the standard-setting process. SOP 78-10 was significant because it was the first time the accounting profession had spoken in any detailed manner to accounting and reporting issues faced by the entire nonprofit sector.

FASB finally introduced in August of 1987 the first standard for financial accounting and reporting specifically applicable to nonprofit organizations: Statement of Financial Accounting Standards (SFAS) No. 93, *Recognition of Depreciation by Not-For-Profit*

Organizations. As its name implies, this statement required all nonprofits to begin generally recognizing depreciation on long-term assets and disclosing depreciation information in external financial statements, if the statements were to be prepared in accordance with GAAP. SFAS No. 93 was a milestone because it was the first of its kind for nonprofit organizations; however, the standard still did not touch on perhaps the most significant difference between nonprofit and for-profit finances: charitable contributions.

In June 1993, nonprofits finally received long-awaited guidance on accounting for contributions when the FASB published SFAS No. 116, *Accounting for Contributions Received and Contributions Made.* At the same time, the FASB published SFAS No. 117, *Financial Statements of Not-For-Profit Organizations.* As a pair, these standards address the most fundamental accounting issues faced by nonprofits.

SFAS No. 116 and No. 117 would be followed by three other FASB nonprofit projects: (1) SFAS No. 124, *Accounting for Certain Investments Held by Not-for-Profit Organizations,* in 1995; (2) SFAS No. 136, *Transfers of Assets to a Not-for-Profit Organization or Charitable Trust That Raises or Holds Contributions for Others,* in 1999; and (3) SFAS No. 164, *Not-for-Profit Entities: Mergers and Acquisitions-Including an Amendment of SFAS No. 142,* in 2009. Finally, as a result of the FASB's codification efforts completed in 2009, all U.S. industry-specific accounting standards for nonprofits can now be located within the FASB's Accounting Standards Codification at Topic 958, *Not-for-Profit Entities.*[4]

In 1979, the Interdenominational Foreign Mission Association (IFMA) published a booklet entitled *Accounting and Financial Reporting Guide for Missionary Organizations.* It was designed to help achieve uniform accounting and financial reporting by missionary organizations in accordance with the AICPA's guidance on generally accepted accounting principles for nonprofit organizations.

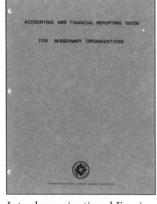

Interdenominational Foreign Mission Association Guide – 1979

ECFA participated in the reporting guide project as part of the Evangelical Joint Accounting Committee (a group of accounting professionals serving Christ-centered ministries) that published the *Accounting and Financial Reporting Guide for Christian Ministries* in 1987. Richard F. "Dick" Capin, CPA and founder of the accounting firm CapinCrouse, was a consultant on the original 1979 booklet and supervised the primary research on the expanded 1987 guide. The guide continued to be updated and enhanced over the years as a financial and accounting resource for

Richard F. Capin

ministries, and with each new edition, ECFA played an important role in its revision, publication, and funding.

Accounting and Financial Reporting Guides for Christian Ministries

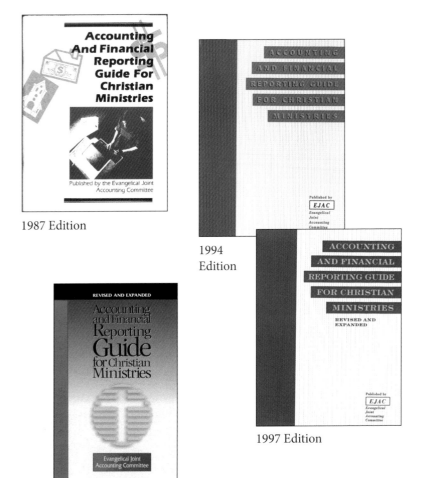

1987 Edition

1994 Edition

1997 Edition

2001 Edition

The latest edition, projected for publication in 2017 by ECFA, will be titled: *The Religious Organization Accounting and Financial Reporting Guide.* Dick's son, Gregg Capin, a partner with CapinCrouse, chaired the committee that developed the 1994, 1997, and 2001 editions of the Guide, as well as actively participated in the development of the forthcoming edition. John Van Drunen, ECFA's executive vice president, and Dick Larkin, serving with BDO, also provided significant leadership for the project.

Gregg Capin

As ECFA grew, it also began an educational program to teach Christ-centered churches and ministries how to be more accountable. The Christian Ministries Management Association, now Christian Leadership Alliance (CLA), was founded on March 20, 1976. In the 1980s, CLA and ECFA sponsored seminars on leadership (CLA) and accountability (ECFA). ECFA has regularly led workshops on accountability issues since that time at CLA national conferences.

Developing ECFA's identity

ECFA's founders wanted people to have widespread confidence in the financial management of all evangelical organizations and to have donors recognize the ECFA seal of approval (Appendix 9) as a symbol of trust. The primary enforcement tools were simple: the application for accreditation, the annual reaccreditation, and special reviews.

A member's accreditation term would be one year in length. Annually, each organization had to be reaccredited. The information required for initial accreditation and annual reaccreditation soon made it clear that ECFA was not merely going to rubber stamp organizations it accredited. Many of ECFA's standards were more stringent than the law. Even leaders on Capitol Hill had not considered requiring nonprofit organizations to have an independent board, much less disclose financial statements to anyone who asked.

During the early years, ECFA depended primarily on the organizations of its board members to help cover operating expenses. World Vision and the Billy Graham Evangelistic Association contributed heavily during that time, since accreditation fees alone were not adequate for even a modest operation.

Any reports of improprieties involving an accredited organization were directed to ECFA's president for review. Minor violations were usually resolved by corrective action by the member. More serious violations could result in an extensive investigation by the Standards Committee and/or board of directors. ECFA's restrictive budget only permitted limited staffing during the early years, so the Standards Committee carried a significant load in enforcing compliance.

Early on, some were worried that ECFA would be a "paper tiger"—unwilling or unable to hold ministries accountable, especially the larger organizations. After all, these were the same organizations whose membership fees paid the bills. There was also fear that the larger organizations would exert too much influence, thus leaving the smaller ministries without a voice. Even Senator Mark Hatfield expressed similar concerns, saying that he had doubts regarding whether ECFA would be able to pass the rigorous test that would inevitably come when faced with the possibility of identifying an organization or group of accredited organizations that failed to meet the standards.

But ECFA met these challenges. The board and Standards Committee knew that confronting a ministry was not something to be done in their own strength, but rather under God's direction and blessing.

The PTL challenge

One glaring example of the lack of compliance with the letter and spirit of ECFA standards was the Praise the Lord Club or People That Love (PTL), headed by Jim and Tammy Bakker. PTL's operations included television programing and a large theme park, Heritage USA. Bakker was a preacher with bases in Charlotte, North Carolina and Fort Mill, South Carolina. PTL was a member of the National Religious Broadcasters during much of the 1980s.

At the time PTL was admitted to ECFA membership, its disqualifying activities were not evident. Over a period of three years, however, ECFA representatives made visits to PTL to review numerous and growing concerns. Rather than come into full compliance, PTL voluntarily withdrew its membership at the end of 1986.

Author Gary Tidwell describes the rise and fall of the PTL ministry in the 1980s:

> With a $52 deposit, Trinity Broadcasting System opened its first bank account in Charlotte, North Carolina on December 7, 1972. Trinity Broadcasting System eventually incorporated in South Carolina as Heritage Village Church and Missionary Fellowship, or "PTL." From this meager $52 beginning, PTL emerged as a major religious organization.
>
> PTL received donations of approximately $400 million from 1982 through 1987. By 1986, PTL claimed it [operated] the third largest theme park in the United States, right behind Disneyland and Disneyworld, and had in excess of six million visitors.
>
> However, despite the outward appearance of financial prosperity, the government would

The *Orange County Register*, February 16, 1986

later contend and prove that Jim Bakker was actually perpetrating a massive wire and mail fraud. The government contended that an overt act of this fraud was the excessive salary and bonuses received by Bakker and select others at PTL. Bakker was ultimately found guilty and sentenced to eight years' imprisonment.

Specifically, Bakker was charged with fraud in the sale of 152,903 fully paid lodging partnerships, providing at least $158 million in revenue for PTL. Beginning in 1984 and continuing until his resignation in March 1987, Bakker and others at PTL continued to solicit its television viewers and mail partners to become a "Lifetime Partner." Generally one could become a PTL lifetime partner for a one-time "gift" of $1,000 to PTL. Each lifetime partner and his immediate family would be able to stay in a luxurious hotel at PTL for four days and three nights, for the balance of the life of the lifetime partner. In addition to making numerous mailed solicitations and almost daily television solicitations concerning the benefits of becoming a lifetime partner, PTL told its followers

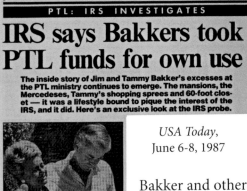

PTL: IRS INVESTIGATES

IRS says Bakkers took PTL funds for own use

The inside story of Jim and Tammy Bakker's excesses at the PTL ministry continues to emerge. The mansions, the Mercedeses, Tammy's shopping sprees and 60-foot closet — it was a lifestyle bound to pique the interest of the IRS, and it did. Here's an exclusive look at the IRS probe.

USA Today,
June 6-8, 1987

that there were limits on the number of people who could become lifetime partners.

For example, Bakker and others said there could only be 25,000 lifetime partners in the Heritage Grand Hotel. However, in reality, at least 66,683 memberships were sold, producing at least $66,900,000. In another PTL hotel (The Towers), Bakker said only 30,000 lifetime partnerships were available, but instead he sold at least 68,755 memberships producing approximately $74,221,751. Furthermore, over $95,100,000 of the total funds received were used for non-construction expenses. . . .

Rather than building the facilities (the Grand Hotel was built and was operational, but The Towers was never completed) and setting aside funds to provide for the obligation to the lifetime partners, PTL drew down the funds almost instantaneously to meet the daily operation expenses. These operational expenses included the executive payroll.

PTL's subsequent bankruptcy on June 12, 1987, and Jim Bakker's criminal conviction for what the government contended was the largest consumer fraud prosecuted as a wire and mail fraud in U.S. history, received extensive publicity. Others at PTL, including Richard Dortch, senior vice president and codefendant with Bakker, were also found guilty of wire and mail fraud. David Taggart, vice president and administrative assistant to Bakker, was convicted of income tax evasion.

In all of the judicial proceedings, compensation of the key executives was one of the focal points of the various trials. Excessive compensation or private inurement was a critical factor in causing the federal bankruptcy judge to hold the Bakkers and David Taggart personally liable to PTL for breaching their fiduciary duty to the corporation.[5]

For the period 1984 to 1987, Jim Bakker's actual compensation was $7,356,478 while his reasonable compensation was $617,717, with the difference of $6,738,761 considered by the court as private inurement.[6]

The PTL debacle gave evidence of the failure of the ministry's governing board. PTL could not afford the bonuses and opulent lifestyle the Bakkers were enjoying. Board members (except Jim Bakker and Richard Dotch) provided court testimony indicating they had no knowledge of the compensation and bonuses paid to Bakkers.[7]

PTL's independent CPAs, Delloitte Haskins and Sells, auditors of PTL from 1977 to 1984, and Laventhol and Horwath, auditors for 1985 and 1986, received their share of criticism for paying compensation to the Bakkers that had not been approved by PTL's full board.[8]

In the spring of 1987, one needed a scorecard to track the players in the evangelism real-life soap opera. Among the participants and events:

- Jim Bakker appeared on his TV network to explain why he had relinquished the reins of his $129 million-a-year PTL empire. It was not because he had confessed to an affair with Jessica Hahn occurring in 1980. Instead, Bakker said he resigned because of a rival evangelist's takeover of his church, including the cable network and the Heritage USA theme park. The PTL cable network was reaching 13.5 million households over 171 stations.

- A rival was Rev. Jimmy Swaggart, a preacher from Baton Rouge, LA, with a substantial U.S. television audience, as well. Swaggart admitted that he had passed along rumors about Bakker's illicit behavior to officials of the Assemblies of God, the denomination in which both were clergy.

- Jerry Falwell, a Lynchburg, VA, pastor, TV personality and university head, was firmly in control of PTL, having taken over the organization at Bakker's behest. At an emergency meeting of the reconstituted PTL board at Heritage USA, Bakker's close aide, Richard Dortch, was installed as president of the organization.

- The very day Dortch became president, the media reported that Dortch had helped negotiate a deal with

Hahn. It was charged that PTL paid $265,000 to Hahn and her advisers to buy her silence.[9]

Following a 16-month federal grand jury probe, Bakker was indicted in 1988 on eight counts of mail fraud, 15 counts of wire fraud, and one count of conspiracy. The jury found him guilty on all 24 counts. While the details of the fraud and conspiracy are long forgotten, the air-conditioned dog house PTL bought for Tammy's Saint Bernard is oft-remembered. Bakker was released from prison on December 1, 1994.

Art Borden from ECFA was called as a witness for the prosecution and also testified at the civil trial. He gave hundreds of interviews to media outlets: *U.S. News and World Report*, radio stations, CNN, and 60 Minutes.

Emerging from the PTL Era

In light of these events, ECFA took a number of proactive steps. It began to more significantly evaluate the organizational structure of applicants and renewals to ensure proper governance. In a Standards Committee report, board member Rollin Van Broekhoven, a Washington, D.C. federal judge who presided over public contract law litigation, stated, "If there is anything that has more completely dominated the agenda of the Standards Committee during 1988, it is the subject of boards and their role in the affairs of the organization."

ECFA's initial standards on fundraising were very basic (Appendix 2). In view of the increasing importance of this issue, however, the Standards Committee labored over a more detailed set of fundraising standards for several years, and they were eventually added to ECFA's standards in 1987 (Appendix 3).

In the wake of the Jim Bakker scandal, the National Religious Broadcasters (NRB) formed a similar accrediting organization called the Ethics and Financial Integrity Commission (EFICOM) in 1988. Its objective was similar to ECFA's—to help insure the integrity and fiscal soundness of broadcast ministries. After a few years, NRB approached ECFA about administering the program and ECFA agreed.[10] As EFICOM developed, many EFICOM members were also ECFA members and vice versa, so having separate organizations was not viable. EFICOM ceased to function separately in 1993.[11] This allowed "NRB to focus its resources on serving rather than policing its members."

Tom McCabe, president of KMA, a direct response marketing and communications consulting firm, served on both the ECFA board and Standards Committee. He said, "In 1986 I was invited to attend a board meeting as an observer with the idea of being invited onto the Standards Committee. I appreciated the quality of the people, the tone of the conversation on issues of possible noncompliance. I

Tom McCabe

thought, 'This is the kind of group we need to build in our genre of Christian fundraising.' My first impression lasted throughout my tenure. I felt it was one of the highlights of my career."[12]

Clarence Reimer (later ECFA acting president/president 1990–1994), who had served as the president of CRISTA Ministries, a charter ECFA member, was hired to participate in the development of Member Evaluation Teams. In 1987, at an ECFA strategic planning meeting, the decision was made to conduct on-site evaluations of ECFA members. These on-site visits were designed to assure greater compliance with the standards, educate members concerning the standards, and strengthen ECFA member relations. Members to be evaluated would be chosen at random.

The new field review program started in 1989 with Clarence Reimer conducting most of the early field reviews. One of his early field review trainees was Dan Busby, who was volunteering as a member of the ECFA Standards Committee. Dan would join the ECFA staff in 1999 and later become its sixth president in 2008.

Bill Altman was one of the professionals who volunteered for service during ECFA's formative years. A highly respected CPA and partner with Ernst & Young, a major international accounting firm, Bill began serving on the Standards Committee in 1985, where he would serve for 12 years. Later, he joined the ECFA staff as Vice President of Compliance and a Field Review Representative, completing 242 one-day field reviews.

Bill Altman

Art Borden resigned as ECFA president in October 1990 and accepted a position with the American Bible Society. Clarence Reimer was named ECFA's acting president.

Because of the way it handled PTL compliance concerns, ECFA gained many new members. The event cast ECFA in a positive light, giving it added status and credibility.

ECFA celebrated its 10th anniversary in 1989 in Washington, D.C.
(L to R) Eldon Howard, Ted Engstrom, George Wilson, Brandt
Gustavson, and Joel Aarsvold

Chapter Four

Facing Challenges

"I was prepared for the worst things
I might encounter seeing the underbelly
of Christian organizations, but less prepared
for the salt-of-the-earth people who would never
do anything to harm the cause of Christ.
They had little notoriety.
They were just there to help people in need.
They were the people that definitely
were inspiring to me."

Paul Nelson, ECFA Former President

In December 1990, the ECFA board appointed Clarence Reimer as interim president. Meanwhile, a nationwide search began to permanently fill the position. Clarence had been a staff member since 1988, serving as director of member review and compliance. His knowledge of ECFA and strong administrative skills resulted in a smooth transition. He was appointed president in 1991.

Clarence Reimer
President (1990–1994)

During this time, the field review program gained momentum. It reinforced ECFA's commitment to full disclosure and accountability, which further enhanced the value of the ECFA seal. The response of the organizations chosen for review was overwhelmingly positive. Most expressed a sincere desire to improve wherever necessary to reflect better management and financial practices.

The initial ECFA standards were intentionally broadly stated (Appendix 2). But as time went by, ECFA realized the standards needed further amplification. Using the expertise of several board and Standards Committee members, ECFA began developing a set of commentaries to the ECFA standards. These were completed in 1991.

Dulles Corner Park, near Dulles International Airport
ECFA had a modest office on the first floor (1992–1999)

In 1992, ECFA produced its first public service announce-ments. These were released nationwide on approximately 200 Christian radio stations. Each was one-minute long. Dr. James Dobson of Focus on the Family narrated, describing the benefits of ECFA membership for both ministries and donors. Listeners were invited to call toll-free for a member list and Giver's Guide. The phones started ringing. Donors were pleased and relieved that ECFA could provide a list of Christian organizations dedicated to appropriate accountability and integrity in both ministry and finance.

On June 15, 1993, Representative J. J. Pickle (D-TX), chairman of the House Subcommittee on Oversight of the Committee on Ways and Means, conducted a hearing on the administration of, and compliance with, the federal tax laws applicable to nonprofits. Tom McCabe, then chairman of the ECFA board, was invited to testify before the subcommittee. He had helped draft the initial ECFA standards and was in an excellent position to describe the standards, review ECFA's procedures, and then comment on proposed legislation. President Clarence Reimer and Gregg Capin joined McCabe as he presented at the hearing.

The Pickle hearings were partly the result of a United Way of America (UWA) scandal in 1991. UWA had, among other things, been accused of paying its CEO excessively, as well as transferring funds to spin-off organizations. The CEO, his family, and top UWA officials had financial interests in these spinoffs. Representative Pickle was planning to introduce legislation which included establishing a reasonable compensation limitation for nonprofit executives.[1]

The UWA generated political debate at both the federal and state levels. While almost all condemned abuse by wrong-doers, not all agreed on the magnitude of the problems or on the appropriate solutions. Who, in fact, governs the nonprofit sector? And who benefits? The consensus of the Pickle hearings narrowed the policy agenda down to two items on which the major players could agree:

- The need for improved public reporting and financial disclosure by nonprofit organizations, and

- Intermediate sanctions (tax penalties that could serve as an alternative to completely revoking the tax-exempt status of noncomplying organizations).

Transitioning Leadership

Meanwhile, ECFA had internal business to address. Clarence Reimer had announced his intention to resign as president, although he agreed to remain on staff until a replacement was found. He had faithfully served in the presidency for four years but was ready to step down.

Paul D. Nelson, executive vice president/chief operating officer with Focus on the Family at the time, was vice chairman of the ECFA board and a member of the Search Committee to replace Clarence. A search firm was engaged, and one after another candidate was interviewed. ECFA's

Paul Nelson
President (1994–2006)

modest budget precluded a compensation package attractive to most candidates. The Search Committee came up empty-handed.

Just after the interview of the final candidate, Paul had a spiritual experience at Focus on the Family. It was during the construction of the ministry's new Colorado Springs headquarters. Each weekend Paul went to the property to check the progress. One particular Sunday afternoon, he climbed the ladder to the top floor. He looked around, saw Pike's Peak in the distance, and then looked at the layout drawn by the architect. He could see all the pieces, all at once, and it was exhilarating. He felt the Spirit stirring his heart and he found himself praying out loud. In that moment, he got the sense that his purpose at Focus was to lead them through the construction of the new building—but perhaps not beyond.

As he recalled, in that particular moment, Paul felt a lifting of the mantle for the first time in his nine years at Focus. Why hadn't the Search Committee been able to find the right candidate for ECFA? Paul talked to his wife, Elaine, prayed about the opportunity, and had begun to ask himself, "If this last person turns us down, does that mean I'm the one to move ECFA forward?"

When the final candidate turned down ECFA's invitation, Paul called Tom McCabe and said, "Tom, I think the Lord is speaking to me. I'd like to resign from the Search Committee and put my name in for consideration for president of ECFA." Shortly thereafter, Paul was elected president.

The New Era Debacle

During Paul's second year as president, he received a telephone call one day while he and Elaine were going on vacation, headed south on Interstate 95 in Virginia. The caller asked if Paul had seen *The Wall Street Journal* that day, the front page breaking the news that The Foundation for New Era Philanthropy, led by John Bennett, had filed for bankruptcy. Paul turned the car around at

THE WALL STREET JOURNAL
TUESDAY, MAY 16, 1995

Crumbling Pyramid

Owing $500 Million, New Era Charity Seeks Refuge From Creditors

Mystery Donors Don't Exist,
Founder Tells His Staff;
Colleges Face Big Losses

A Big Blow to Good Works

the next exit. He knew enough about New Era to know this was a very big deal and could severely impact some ECFA members.

In an enlightening case study on New Era, Niles Logue writes,

> Bennett, affectionately called Jack by colleagues and friends, was the consummate "Main Line" Philadelphian. While not wealthy . . . he was nevertheless connected, urbane, effective—a doer and charismatic—a leader. A former administrator of a substance abuse program during the '70s and '80s, he acquired a reputation for helping [nonprofits] develop their financial and management infra-structures, including development of effective

fundraising skills and strategies through his consulting firm, Human Resource Management.[1]

In 1982 he formed the Center for New Era Philanthropy to assist foundations in their screening and vetting of tentative charities.[2]

By 1989, the organization had morphed into the Foundation for New Era Philanthropy (New Era). New Era

offered fundraising consultation through the Templeton Institute and a matching gift program with the expectation that the funds of a nonprofit would be doubled in six months.

Nonprofits desiring to participate in the matching fund had to be nominated by individual philanthropists. Nominated organizations had to submit an exhaustive application, leaving the impression that the matching funds were only available to a select few nonprofits.[3]

Elusive grandeur: New Era literature tried to appeal to an elite crowd.

"The structure of [Bennett's] scheme (double your money every six months) required cash inflow to quadruple every year in order to sustain the grant-matching payouts to participating beneficiary donors, and the cash demands would exceed these levels at times because the cash inflows would naturally be uneven."[4] Initially, Bennett devised a kiting plan involving at least six checking accounts. But this was a short-term fix, so he moved onto something more elaborate. He created a pyramid scheme.

He began by asking several friends to invest $5,000 as "beneficiary donors." He told them an anonymous donor would double their money after three months and distribute it to the charity of their choice. He had started by limiting participants to individual donors, then included nonprofits in 1994.

Needing a broker to handle the deposits, he opened an account with Prudential Securities, telling investors that it was a "quasi-escrow" account. In reality, funds were comingled and Bennett frequently tapped into them. With these large sums on deposit, Bennett was able to open a $45 million margin account (much like a line of credit) to draw upon as needed. Certainly, the Prudential name helped Bennett in soliciting funds, but even more reassuring was the toll-free New Era telephone number staffed by Prudential employees to field questions from current and prospective New Era investors.

As in all Ponzi schemes, it soon became necessary to keep increasing the amount received from donors and/or investors—$5,000, then $25,000, to $50,000 and up, and the waiting period increased to six, nine, or even ten months. The mysterious anonymous donors grew to nine. He was able to keep his promise to double the investors' money by using the money of later investors and borrowing heavily on his credit line at Prudential Securities. Plus, he paid brokers to bring in deposits from charities.

His scheme became an enormous success as he kept expanding the number of investors, raising the investment amounts, and even opening offices overseas in London and Hong Kong. But soon it would all come crashing down.

New Era hit a ceiling in 1995 as growth in inflows had slowed to an estimated annualized rate of 230 percent, which was inadequate to maintain the fraud. "Suddenly in late 1994 and 1995 endowment money was solicited with a match period of nine months. The nine months would slow the revenue growth required to sustain the pyramid from 400 percent per annum to 250 percent. Then, on April 24, 1995, in a move of clear desperation to improve cash flow, Bennett announced a sweeter deal—a new fund that would pay out $2.50 for every $1 deposited after a ten-month period."[5] To cover grant payments due in early May, Bennett took his margin account at Prudential up to $48 million.

New Era purported to have a board of directors. However, on New Era's 1992 Form 990, Bennett was listed as the sole director. The amended 1993 Form 990 lists five other individuals as directors. Dr. John M. Templeton, Jr. was one of the five listed as a director. When he was later

Federal Grand Jury Indicts Founder of New Era Philanthropy Fund

John Bennett, founder of the Foundation for New Era Philanthropy, leaves the federal courthouse in Philadelphia with his daughter after he was indicted on 82 counts of fraud and other criminal activities.

interviewed, he said that he "never served on the board, and (he doesn't) remember being invited."[6]

Bennett said he never took a salary from New Era. However, it was

On the witness stand: New Era's founder, John G. Bennett, Jr., with Bible in hand, breaks down at his September sentencing hearing in a Philadelphia federal courtroom.

estimated that Bennett diverted some $5 million to other controlled companies and another $3.5 million to his personal needs, including $620,000 for his new home, over the six years New Era operated.[7]

Albert J. Meyer, an accounting professor at Spring Arbor College, took a personal interest in New Era The college invested several millions into New Era.[8] He began to investigate possible fraud issues at New Era in July 1993. Meyer persevered in his investigation even while being pressured by Spring Arbor's leaders and others to stand down. He is generally credited with exposing the pyramid scheme and bringing it to a halt.

A tip to the Securities and Exchange Commission (SEC) initiated a federal inquiry into Prudential Securities. That inquiry led to lightning-fast action that ended the age of New Era and John Bennett. On Thursday, May 11, 1995, Prudential sued New Era and froze its assets to cover approximately $50 million in borrowed funds.

New Era had to file for Chapter 13 bankruptcy. (Four days later, the court changed the Chapter 13 filing to a Chapter 7 liquidation proceeding.) The bankruptcy filing stated that New Era had estimated its assets at $80 million but owed up to $551 million. There were 300 unsecured creditors listed in the filing. At that time, it was the largest single bankruptcy in the nonprofit sector in U.S. history.

On May 13, 1995, Bennett went before his staff and stunned them by confessing that there were no anonymous donors, and on May 15, 1995, he had his attorneys file for bankruptcy.[9]

On May 18, 1995, the SEC sued Bennett and New Era, accusing them of fraudulently offering and selling unregistered securities. The SEC also charged that Bennett diverted $4.2 million from donors and charities to other entities he controlled.

ECFA Responds

Many ECFA member organizations were impacted by New Era, and ECFA quickly responded to the bankruptcy. At a meeting in Atlanta on May 18, 1995, this group of members formed a task force called United Response to New Era (United Response). It would enable all organizations, large and small, to benefit from shared legal strategies and counsel, financial solutions, understanding of bankruptcy proceedings, and enhanced communications. The group appointed ECFA to lead United Response and federal judge Rollin Van Broekhoven as the chair of United Response. Rollin served on the ECFA board for 15 years, plus many

years on the Standards Committee. He
was elected ECFA's board chair just six
weeks prior to the collapse of New Era.

Rollin Van
Broekhoven

United Response developed seven
biblical principles, the essence being
that if ministries received a net gain
from New Era, they should voluntarily
return the money to charities that lost
money (exceptions would be granted
for charities with extenuating circum-
stances). They reasoned that keeping the money could not
be biblically defended.

The bankruptcy court scheduled a creditors' meeting in
Philadelphia for June 26, 1995. United Response and others
met beforehand to agree on a consensus candidate as the
permanent bankruptcy trustee. The creditors overwhelmingly elected the Honorable Judge Arlin Adams to
the position. (Adams was a former judge on the Third U.S.
Circuit Court of Appeals.) The decision was not automatic—
far from it. There were more than 400 attorneys present,
each trying to protect the interests of their clients.

There were those who said that ECFA should not get
involved—after all, there could be liability for ECFA, and
ECFA had not invested any money. It was not part of
ECFA's mission. But if not ECFA, then who?

Following the June 26 meeting, the focus was to propose and
negotiate a global settlement, which could be accepted by
some 3,000 creditors and others. This required many draft

proposals and a great deal of negotiation between members of the bankruptcy bar, Van Broekhoven, lawyers representing creditors, debtors, and major donors or philanthropists. Van Broekhoven met daily with both Judge Adams and his attorneys to devise the settlement.

At last, a year later, on August 22, 1996, Judge Arlin Adams approved a settlement returning at least $39 million to institutions that had lost money in the collapse of New Era. As impressive as the size of the settlement was, more impressive was the large percentage of the loss recovered— almost unheard of—and the speed and cooperation with which the resolution was reached. In 1997, faced with four lawsuits accusing it of negligence in its dealings with Bennett, Prudential Securities agreed to settle by paying $18 million. Charities would ultimately recover more than 93% of the total funds lost.

As the United Response legal bills began to build, funds were needed to cover them. The amount would eventually reach more than $600,000. Again Ted Engstrom, now board member emeritus, lent his considerable support, reputation, and influence to help. In an appeal dated August 9, 1995, he asked more than 250 ministries, foundations, and individuals to contribute toward the cost of the legal bills. The funds came in—like manna—leaving only $5,000 unpaid of the total amount owed.

So many ministries demonstrated a beautiful Christian spirit during the New Era debacle. Some not even directly affected offered assistance.

John Bennett was indicted on 82 counts, under which he could have faced 907 years in jail and $28 million in damages. He was charged with laundering money, in part to:

- Use $571,465 to buy a new home,

- Give $227,000 for a house for his daughter,

- Spend $53,206 to buy a Lexus automobile, and

- Pay $49,350 for air travel from Philadelphia to New Zealand for himself and family members.

Bennett's lawyers argued that he suffered brain damage from two auto accidents, causing him to "hear voices in his head that told him New Era was part of a divine plan."[10] However, he was convicted and sentenced to federal prison in March 1997. Just prior to his sentencing in a Philadelphia courtroom, Bennett said, "As the years passed by, the desire became a dream, the dream became a need, the need became an obsession, the obsession became a fantasy, and the fantasy became a delusion."[11] He served 11 years and was released in March 2008.

Chapter Five

Expanding Impact

> "I judge all things
> only by the price they shall gain
> in eternity."
>
> John Wesley

In 1998, wheels were placed in motion leading to ECFA's relocation from Dulles Corner Park to Winchester, Virginia in 1999. ECFA's 10-year lease was about to expire and the high-technology surge in the Dulles airport area made office space very expensive. A lease renewed could come at double or triple the cost. Additionally, an anticipated staff turnover from retirement and motherhood provided an excellent opportunity for ECFA to consider leaving the Dulles airport area.

Access to Capitol Hill was essential, but an outlying community would still provide adequate access. Moreover, it would mean significant savings for ECFA's office and staff.

Paul Nelson began searching for a new location in a radius around Dulles airport. Possible locations included Warrenton, Virginia, and a former Army base at Vint Hill, Virginia. But a new condominium office building in the burgeoning city of Winchester, one hour west of Dulles airport, soon became the focus. Winchester had all the services ECFA needed, while remaining in close proximity to Washington, D.C. A deal was finalized, and the build-out of the new office was completed in August 1999. Paul and Elaine Nelson moved to be near the new headquarters, and Winchester-based personnel were hired to staff the new office.

In 1999, Dan Busby joined the ECFA staff as vice president of member and donor services. Dan was no stranger to ECFA, having served as a volunteer on the Standards Committee for eight years. He was a nationally recognized speaker and an author. His articles had appeared in many publications, and he was a contributing writer for several commentaries concerning the ECFA standards. He had conducted numerous ECFA field reviews pro bono before joining the staff, and would go on to conduct over 300 one-day reviews of

Office in Winchester, VA (1999–Present)—
ECFA offices are part of the lower level

members. At Paul Nelson's retirement dinner in 2006, Paul said that his greatest contribution to ECFA was his recruiting and eventual hiring of Dan Busby.

When Dan joined the staff, ECFA had hosted a limited number of workshops to promote its triad of principles: good governance, sound financial management, and ethical fundraising practices/stewardship. With his professional background and speaking skills, ECFA rapidly expanded its educational offerings through regional workshops and at national conventions.

Spreading the word

Also in 1998, ECFA developed its first website: www.ECFA.org. While it was very basic, listing only the current accredited members and reflecting ECFA's standards, it was a sound start into the world of the Internet.

Early in his presidency, Paul Nelson had recognized the need to develop standardized information on many issues related to ECFA's foundational principles. Paul knew a series of brief expository documents explaining the basics of these issues was needed. These resources would also point church and nonprofit leaders to additional reference materials.

This research and writing project was one of Dan's early assignments at ECFA. He had already written on many of these topics in his two tax and finance books published annually by Zondervan since 1991; he was well prepared to tackle the assignment.

The information on governance, financial management, and stewardship/fundraising issues was initially developed in written form and faxed on request. Then, as the website evolved, ECFA began to post this information online. This was the beginning of ECFA's Knowledge Center, which would grow to hundreds of documents and be accessed hundreds of thousands of times over the ensuing years—plus becoming the basis for many electronic booklets. After 2000, a member profile was also added to the website reflecting financial and other data for each member.

Growing ECFA's influence amid increased nonprofit oversight

On September 12 and 13, 1999, ECFA held a 20th anniversary celebration in Washington, D.C. Approximately 200 representatives of ECFA-member organizations attended. Dr. Ravi Zacharias was a plenary speaker. Awards were presented to honor the early supporters and founders of ECFA: Billy Graham, Ted Engstrom, George Wilson, and Rollin Van Broekhoven.

Unfortunately, it was not long until scandal again reared its ugly head. That same year, the Baptist Foundation of Arizona, a non-ECFA member, declared bankruptcy after state regulators found it lacked the money to cover its debts to investors. The Foundation provided trust and endowment management services for Southern Baptist Convention entities in Arizona. The Foundation—with assets between $160 and $200 million—owed nearly $600 million to more than 13,000 investors to whom it had promised lucrative returns.[1]

(L to R) Crawford Loritts, Jr. and Dennis Rainey
at the 20th anniversary celebration—
both have served on ECFA's board

The scandals started piling up. The former head of the Hale House for Children, a non-ECFA member, was forced to resign her position in 2001 amid allegations of financial improprieties. She and her husband faced criminal charges for stealing more than a million dollars from the charity.[2] And the Tampa-based Greater Ministries International, another non-ECFA member, reportedly ran a Ponzi scheme, taking nearly $500 million from 18,000 individuals. In both cases, the suspect transactions had been going on for years before they became known to most board members and to outside investigators.[3]

The terrorist destruction on American soil on September 11, 2001, had a significant impact on ECFA's accredited organizations. The 9/11 events rocked the U.S. economy.

Donors became cautious in their giving because of a prevailing sense of fear. It took several years for ECFA's members to work through that financial impact.

In 2001 and 2002, a number of major corporate and accounting scandals, including those affecting Enron, Tyco International, and Adelphia University, resulted in passage of the 2002 Sarbanes-Oxley Act. This legislation covered issues such as auditor independence, corporate governance, internal control assessment, and enhanced financial disclosure.

While Sarbanes-Oxley focused almost exclusively on the for-profit sector, it was a wake-up call for the nonprofit sector as well. There was a renewed realization that nonprofits must protect the confidence of their constituents.

Each scandal, each threatening event affected donors' trust in charities. Organizations accredited by ECFA were more readily trusted, and as time went on, each episode made it clearer and clearer that donors needed a source of trust for nonprofits, including Christ-centered organizations.

"In 2003, noting that Christian organizations tended to use secular fundraising methods with little consideration of whether these practices were consistent with God's Word, Dr. Wesley Willmer convened a national task force under the joint auspices of the Christian Stewardship Association (CSA) and ECFA to address this concern. The task force consisted of 23 Christian leaders,

Wesley K. Willmer
ECFA Senior Vice President
2009–2011

including three with experience as seminary presidents." The task force developed the *Biblical Principles for Stewardship and Fundraising.*[4]

History began repeating itself in the summer of 2004. At that time, the Senate Finance Committee, chaired by Senator Charles Grassley (R-IA), began to hold hearings on abuses in the charitable community. The abuses related to tax-shelter loopholes, car donation programs, and several highly publicized scandals involving well-known national charities. ECFA again became fully engaged with the Senate Finance Committee, which voiced its concerns and opinions to ECFA in a private meeting.

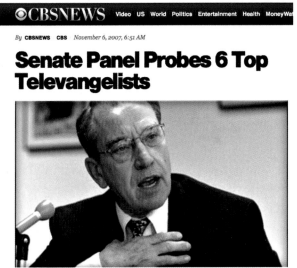

⊙ **CBSNEWS** Video US World Politics Entertainment Health MoneyWat

By **CBSNEWS** **CBS** *November 6, 2007, 6:51 AM*

Senate Panel Probes 6 Top Televangelists

Charles Grassley, US Senator from Iowa, May 3, 2001 **AP**

While some of the resulting proposals were merely extensions of the Sarbanes-Oxley legislation, many represented excessive intrusion into the affairs of ministries. This was another significant opportunity for ECFA, with its credible voice, to speak out on nonprofit tax policy issues within its sphere of influence.

Due in part to ECFA's growing reputation, Paul Nelson was named to a 25-member Panel on the Nonprofit Sector (Panel). This Panel was convened by Independent Sector[5] at the request of Senator Grassley to advise the Finance Committee regarding charity oversight legislation to be introduced in 2005.

The Senate proposals, breathtaking in scope, were suggested in response to a variety of real and perceived abuses—some resulting from high-profile media reports that got the attention of members of Congress. In one of the subcommittee groups related to the Panel, a key congressional staffer said to an ECFA representative, "*Your* group is not the problem." What a testimony!

Four of ECFA's top leaders, (L to R) Paul Nelson,
Clarence Reimer, Art Borden, Olan Hendrix

Paul Nelson retired as ECFA president in March 2006, but he continued to serve on the Panel for a year after his retirement until the Panel's work was completed. Ultimately, the Panel recommended 29 principles for self-regulation, generally consistent with ECFA's standards.

Ken Behr, a former Ford Motor Company sales executive and staff member of an ECFA member church, North Way Christian Community, Wexford, PA, assumed leadership of ECFA on May 1, 2006. During his tenure, Ken enthusiastically promoted ECFA. He worked to stretch ECFA and generated a number of ideas about how to grow the organization. He also pushed to use technology more fully in providing membership and educational services.

Ken Behr
President (2006–2008)

Major improvements to ECFA's website were introduced in 2007. The first posting began of current news about church and nonprofit governance, financial management, and stewardship/fundraising issues—what would later become the popular "In the News" section of the website.

The initial commentaries on ECFA standards had several primary authors and had been written over a period of about 20 years. In 2007, Dan Busby led a project to rewrite the commentaries from a common viewpoint, plus subjecting them to review from a theological perspective. The commentaries were then published for the first time in booklet form.

Also that year, ECFA made a major revision in its standards. The change remained well within the original charter, but was intended to include more organizations.

A primary requirement for accreditation had always been an annual audit of financial statements. Because of significant increases in the cost of audits by CPAs (following Sarbanes-Oxley and other corporate reforms), ECFA began to accept financial statement compilations or reviews for those organizations with more modest revenues.[6] It was clear that the cost of audits would continue to rise and become increasingly difficult for smaller churches and nonprofits to fund. This strategic decision helped ensure that quality organizations of all sizes could continue to qualify for ECFA accreditation.

Chapter Six

Moving to a Higher Level

> "We have to be braver than we think we can be,
> because God is constantly calling us
> to be more than we are."
>
> Madeleine L'Engle

Through the years, each ECFA president has brought his own leadership gifts to his tenure.

In April 2008, Dan Busby was appointed acting president

Dan Busby
Vice President
(1999–2008)
President (2008–Present)

following Ken Behr's resignation, and he was elected president in February 2009 after ECFA's board conducted a national search. He was uniquely qualified for the job, having served ECFA for the previous 20 years, ten as a member of the Standards Committee and ten more on staff in senior leadership positions.

As Dan assumed ECFA's presidency, he recognized ECFA was primarily known

for financial accountability issues. While there had been some focus on resource-raising, more needed to be done in this area. Governance was at the heart of nearly every member compliance issue, yet ECFA had only provided limited governance education to its members.
Dan pledged to change this—leading to webinars, Knowledge Center documents, videos, Governance Toolboxes, member surveys, books (print and electronic), and more to cover not only financial management but also resource-raising and governance.

John Van Drunen
Director of Compliance
(2008–2009)
Vice President
(2008–2014)
Executive Vice President
(2015–Present)

In 2008, John Van Drunen joined ECFA as director of compliance. An attorney and a CPA, he raised the technical and administrative capacity of ECFA far beyond what it had enjoyed before. Promoted to vice president in 2010 and executive vice president in 2015, John provided oversight for ECFA's compliance program, co-authored books with Dan Busby, and presented workshops at regional and national conferences. In 2012, he served as the project manager of ECFA's office expansion.

Kim Sandretzky
Director of
Communications
(2012–2014)
Vice President of
Communications
(2015–Present)

Kim Sandretzky, with past experience as an overseas missionary, also joined the ECFA team in 2008. She was promoted to director of communications in 2012, and again to vice president of communications in 2015, where she helped ECFA reach new levels of excellence in its promotion of special events, webinars, and many other programs.

Michael Martin
Director of Member
Services and Legal
Counsel (2012–2014)
Vice President
(2015–Present)

Another key staff addition occurred in 2012 when attorney Michael Martin joined the staff. Michael used his gifts handling in-house counsel responsibilities, member services, the compliance program, public speaking, and co-authored books with Dan Busby and John Van Drunen. He was promoted to vice president in 2015, and led the launch of ECFA's church membership initiative in 2016.

Responding to new opportunities

Meanwhile, the Internal Revenue Service had designed a new and significantly expanded version of Form 990, the annual reporting form required by most nonprofits other than churches. An early draft indicated the IRS would ask for much more information than in the past, especially for ministries with international activities. Because disclosure of a ministry's staff, location, activities, or beneficiaries in certain countries (or even domestically in some cases) could endanger persons, ECFA proactively opposed public disclosure of this highly sensitive information. As a result, ECFA and other organizations were successful in obtaining a delay (a delay that is still in place to this day) in this proposed change to information reporting.

In late 2008, ECFA launched an online service called ServantMatch® for its accredited organizations and givers supporting them. Donors were quick to use this web-based tool in finding ECFA-accredited organizations to support. ServantMatch® allows donors to view all ECFA members with related giving opportunities, according to ministry sectors and categories. In conjunction with online member

profile pages, it helps donors determine if a ministry is accredited by ECFA, understand its mission, review important financial information, and then be linked directly to the charity's website. While ECFA does not process gifts generated by ServantMatch®, anecdotal information suggests that millions of dollars in gifts for Kingdom purposes have been generated through this avenue.

As a result of its continuing growth, ECFA needed greater efficiencies for processing membership applications and annual renewals. A project began in 2008 to allow for online submission of application and renewal information. These steps helped ECFA administer its programs without significantly increasing staffing/costs commensurate with its rapid growth in membership during this era.

In 2010, ECFA's database was used as the basis for the first annual State of Giving Report, which soon attracted national media attention because it represented the most significant giving data for evangelical organizations available. Issued each fall, this report is often contrasted with the data from studies of nonprofits in other sectors.

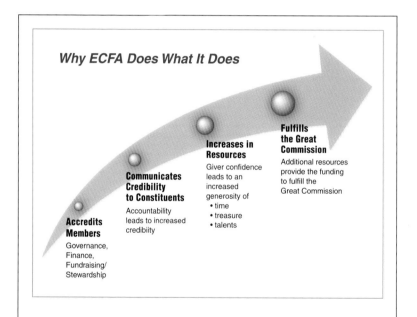

Why ECFA Does What It Does

Accredits Members
Governance, Finance, Fundraising/ Stewardship

Communicates Credibility to Constituents
Accountability leads to increased credibiity

Increases in Resources
Giver confidence leads to an increased generosity of
• time
• treasure
• talents

Fulfills the Great Commission
Additional resources provide the funding to fulfill the Great Commission

Organizations generally do not become members because of *what* ECFA does, or *how* ECFA does it, but because of *why* ECFA does it. The *how* must be done by ECFA with excellence. The *what* ECFA does—setting and applying standards—is vital. But it is the *why* that makes all the difference: accrediting members, which communicates trust to supporters, which increases resources, which helps fulfill the Great Commission.

Also in 2010, technology allowed ECFA to begin offering webinars as part of its educational program—a robust series of church and nonprofit online seminars on governance, financial management, and fundraising/stewardship-related topics. The series immediately became popular and allows ECFA to serve thousands of participants each year from the Winchester, VA office.

After two years of study, in 2011, revisions to ECFA's standards and commentaries were approved. The modifications represented the most thorough updating of the standards since the fundraising standards had been added in 1989. The revisions included making the language of the standards equally relevant to churches and ministries. The revised standards also paved the way for certain non-creedal ministries to join ECFA, based on their commitment to the entire Word of God in lieu of their own statement of faith or commitment to ECFA's statement of faith.

The first annual Governance Survey was conducted of ECFA members in 2011. This project was the precursor to annual financial management and stewardship/fundraising surveys, expanding the surveys of ECFA members on trends and best practices.

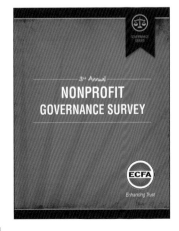

By 2011, ECFA had fully utilized its office space. The Lord provided, and the adjoining space on the lower level of the

(L to R) Art Borden, Dan Busby, and Paul Nelson
at the October 2012 dedication of the new office space in Winchester, VA.

two-story office building at 440 West Jubal Early Drive in
Winchester, VA was acquired. This expansion more than
doubled physical capacity. It provided the space needed to
facilitate a growing number of members and the expanding
services offered to them.

ECFA continued to increase its impact for integrity and
high-quality ministry administration with online learning
opportunities focused on governance, financial management, and fundraising/stewardship. During 2012 and 2013,
ECFA provided the following expanded services and
products:

✦ At this point in its history, ECFA related, through its
members, to over 20,000 board members. The
significant need for board training was apparent.

A decision was made to launch a series of video-based training tools specifically for boards. The concept: a 10-minute video accompanied by a 10-minute discussion guide for each board member, plus a facilitator's guide.

The first Governance Toolbox, *Recruiting Board Members*, was released during this time frame. In the ensuing years, Governance Toolboxes were released on the following topics: *Balancing Board Roles* and *Conflicts of Interest*.

From 2008–15, ECFA's accredited membership burgeoned, growing faster than at any time in its 36-year history—in spite of the United States being in the depths of a recessionary environment. Nevertheless, it was clear that most churches and other Christ-centered organizations would never become accredited by ECFA—primarily because of their modest size. This was the impetus to spawn ChurchWise.org and NonprofitWise.org, offering a basic level of educational information and training for nonmembers. This web-based concept allows ECFA to share some of its resources with thousands of churches and nonprofits, helping them to achieve a higher level of proficiency in governance, financial management, and fundraising/stewardship.

✦ In 2013, ECFA published two booklets under the newly created ECFAPress brand: *Charitable Giving Guide for Missionaries and Other Workers* and *Charitable Giving Guide for Short-Term Missions Trips.*

In 2016, two booklets were added to this series: *Charitable Giving Guide for Giver-Restricted Gifts* and *Charitable Giving Guide for Acknowledging and Reporting Charitable Gifts.*

✦ An initial series of iBooks™ was published in English and
  Spanish. These products, available in the iTunes™ store
  at no charge, become a great way to broadly distribute
  ECFA-related learning materials.

✦ The two popular guides authored by Dan Busby since
  1992, *Zondervan Minister's Tax
  & Financial Guide* and *Church
  and Nonprofit Tax & Financial
  Guide*, continued to be
  updated and published
  annually. John Van
  Drunen became a
  co-author of the books
  in 2010, with Michael
  Martin joining Dan and
  John as a co-author for
  the 2013 and subsequent
  editions. The 2016

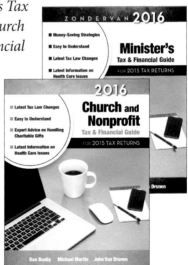

editions marked the 25th consecutive year both books were published.

In 1980, ECFA had 150 founding members. By 2015, the number of accredited organizations exceeded 2,000. There has been a net positive membership gain in every year of ECFA's existence. To God be the glory!

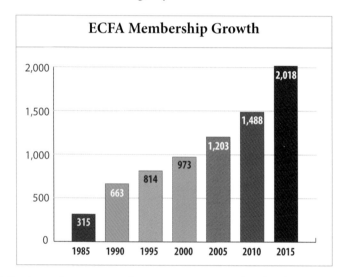

While it took 22 years for ECFA to accredit the first 1,000 members, it took only 14 years to reach the second 1,000.

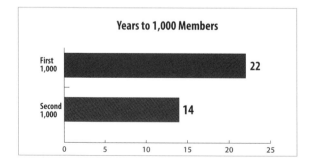

Chapter Seven

The Commission Era

> "ECFA's participation in the Commission is
> very much on mission—as on mission as it can get.
> First, ECFA exists for the very purpose of
> addressing financial integrity and accountability
> and good board governance for its members.
> It exists for the purpose of fostering policy
> that allows for integrity in the form of
> self-regulation and accreditation
> without burdensome government regulation.
> That's what we exist to do."
>
> Michael E. Batts, ECFA Board Member
> and Commission Chairman

ECFA's growing reputation for financial integrity among government leaders came to the fore as members of Congress sharpened their scrutiny of financial abuses, both real and perceived, within nonprofit organizations.

In October 2007, Dan Busby and ECFA board member Michael Batts met with Senator Charles Grassley, then-Ranking Member of the Senate Finance Committee, to share their belief that the tax law needed to provide protections for nonprofit organizations conducting programs in high-risk areas of the world. (The Internal Revenue Service had proposed asking questions on forms subject to public disclosure that could lead to revealing the identity of individuals working in countries closed to the Gospel.) After the discussion was completed, the senator's lead attorney, Dean Zerbe, turned to the senator and asked, "Shall we tell the folks from ECFA about the letters to the churches?" (Dan and Michael quickly surmised he was not talking about Paul's letters to the New Testament churches.) The senator agreed.

Mr. Zerbe then shared that the senator was planning to send letters to six prominent media ministries, organized as churches: Randy and Paula White of Without Walls International Church and Paula White Ministries of Tampa, FL; Benny Hinn of World Healing Center Church, Inc. and Benny Hinn Ministries of Grapevine, TX; David and Joyce Meyer of Joyce Meyer Ministries of Fenton, MO; Kenneth and Gloria Copeland of Kenneth Copeland Ministries of Newark, TX; Bishop Eddie Long of New Birth Missionary Baptist Church and Bishop Eddie Long Ministries of Lithonia, GA; and Creflo and Taffi Dollar of World Changers Church International and Creflo Dollar Ministries of College Park, GA—the ministries would later be dubbed "The Grassley Six." The letters went out in the following weeks, asking the ministries to supply a plethora of detailed financial information.[1]

Some of the ministries responded with information; some did not. Subpoenas were threatened, but not issued. Of the six ministries investigated, only Joyce Meyer Ministries applied, and was approved, for ECFA accreditation.

Fast forward three years to December 17, 2010—when Senator Grassley's then lead attorney, Theresa Pattara, emailed Michael Batts and Dan Busby to set up a conference call later that day. During the call, they learned that the senator wanted to close the investigation while he was still the ranking member of the Senate Finance Committee (his term of service was to end in early January 2011). The senator wanted ECFA's help in responding to the issues and questions raised by his staff. ECFA's leaders rose to the challenge and readily agreed to accept the responsibility.

Senator Grassley's staff issued a formal invitation to ECFA to facilitate responses to 61 pages of tax, accountability, and policy issues. He asked ECFA to provide responses to each of these issues and offer recommendations that would not require burdensome legislation. On January 5, 2011, the senator wrote: "ECFA has a proven track record of accountability with its member organizations and is uniquely situated to work with representatives from the religious and broader nonprofit community. The Panel on the Nonprofit Sector, spearheaded by Independent Sector, provided invaluable feedback to my staff's 2004 proposals regarding charity reform. ECFA's work will be just as vital in informing me and making a positive difference in the religious community."[2]

In response, ECFA formed the Commission on Accountability and Policy for Religious Organizations (Commission).[3] Its purpose was to conduct a multi-year study on whether these issues could be addressed without burdensome legislation.

The Commission would be an independent effort, completely separate from the senator and his staff, privately funded, and autonomous with respect to the IRS.

Michael Batts chaired the ECFA Standards Committee and served on the ECFA board of directors at that time. He was asked to lead the Commission project. As the president and managing partner with the CPA firm of Batts Morrison Wales & Lee, P.A., he was uniquely qualified to take on this major responsibility, having both a passion for nonprofit ministry integrity and a deep knowledge of tax law, regulations, and nonprofit governance.

Michael E. Batts

Again, the same issue was raised that was asked at the time of New Era—is the Commission project within ECFA's mission? Batts was very clear in his response:

> ECFA's participation in the Commission is very much "on mission"—as "on mission" as it can get. First, ECFA exists for the very purpose of addressing financial integrity and accountability and good board governance for its members. It exists for the purpose of fostering policy that allows for integrity in the form of self-regulation and accreditation without burdensome government regulation. That's what we exist to do.

> For the first time in its history, ECFA was requested by the ranking member of the Senate Finance Committee to take on these policy questions and advise him.

He trusted ECFA because of its demonstrated history of integrity. So the answer to the question "Is this a place where ECFA should be?" is "Well, it's either involve ourselves or become spectators. No one was comfortable with being a spectator."

ECFA is uniquely positioned to address these issues. And while there's no assurance that its recommendations will be followed, it will give ECFA the opportunity to evaluate these issues in a manner that is thoughtful, careful, deliberate, professional, and done with much prayer. It is the deep hope of ECFA that it will be one of the great moments in ECFA history—the opportunity to provide meaningful input into these areas that will really make a positive difference for the Kingdom.[4]

On April 13, 2011, ECFA Board Chairman Mark Holbrook named 14 national Christian leaders to serve on the Commission. On September 8, 2011, Commission Chairman Michael Batts named 66 members to one of three panels—a Panel of Legal Experts, a Panel of Religious Sector Representatives, and a Panel of Nonprofit Sector Representatives. They were all widely respected leaders representing the legal profession, every major faith group, and various elements of the nonprofit sector. Their wisdom and participation was essential.

The Panel of Religious Sector Representatives included leaders from nearly every major faith group in America. Special emphasis was placed on engaging leaders who represented large segments of their faith group.

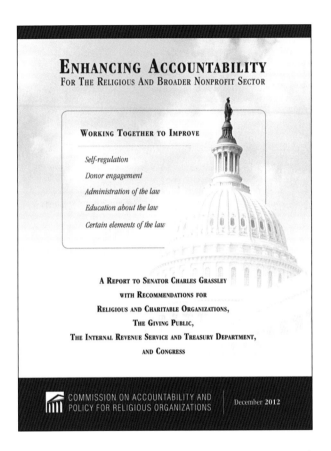

In addition to the Panels' participation, the Commission also received input from the IRS and a virtual town hall meeting, as well as other informal channels.

The Commission's first report was issued in December 2012, *Enhancing Accountability for the Religious and Broader Nonprofit Sector,* and revolved around several central questions:

- Should churches and other nonprofits be more accountable to the federal government?

- Should the rules for determining the reasonableness of nonprofit executive compensation be tightened?

- Is legislation needed to curb perceived abuses of the clergy housing allowance exclusion?

- Should penalties be expanded for nonprofits and their leaders who engage in prohibited activities?

After the first report was released, Senator Grassley commended ECFA and the Commission for their work and

Michael Batts and Dan Busby present the first Commission Report to Senator Charles Grassley in his office, December 2012

noted that the Commission's recommendations should be
considered by Congress in the future when embarking on
comprehensive tax reform.

The Commission's second report, *Government Regulation
of Political Speech by Religious and Other 501(c)(3)
Organizations: Why the Status Quo Is Untenable and
Proposed Solutions*, was released in August 2013. The report
related to another question raised by Senator Grassley not
directly related to the original Grassley Six investigation:

Should the current prohibition against nonprofits' intervention in political campaigns be repealed or modified?

Michael Batts explained the significance of the Commission's work on the political expression issue in his Chairman's message:

> No freedoms are more central to the American experience than the freedom of speech and the freedom to exercise religion. To ensure that we are all reminded of those most fundamental freedoms, the American people enshrined them at the top of the Bill of Rights—the First Amendment to the Constitution of the United States of America.
>
> In light of our knowledge of and rights to such freedoms, it is both disturbing and chilling that the federal government regulates the speech of religious organizations and other organizations dedicated to improving the lives of people. As Americans, we know this instinctively. Yet, since 1954, federal tax law has included a provision that, as currently interpreted and applied, does exactly that. The prohibition against participation or intervention in a political campaign included in Section 501(c)(3) of the Internal Revenue Code prohibits communications that involve support of or opposition to candidates for political office by religious and other 501(c)(3) organizations. It is the only law of its type on the books . . . the only law that allows the Internal Revenue Service to evaluate the content of a sermon delivered by a member of the clergy . . . the only law that could cause a church to lose

its federal tax exemption based on the words spoken by its leaders in a worship service. Federal government officials also know instinctively that the law, as currently interpreted and applied, is problematic— which is why the law is largely unenforced in some respects and inconsistently enforced in others.

The law prohibiting political campaign participation and intervention by 501(c)(3) organizations as currently applied and administered lacks clarity, integrity, respect, and consistency. Guidance from the Internal Revenue Service states that all the "facts and circumstances" must be taken into consideration in determining whether an organization's activities constitute prohibited conduct. Consequently, religious and nonprofit leaders are never quite sure where the lines of demarcation are, and the practical effect of such vagueness is to chill free speech—often in the context of exercising religion. Many 501(c)(3) organizations engage regularly in communications that the IRS says are prohibited, and there are no consequences. Yet, the IRS does enforce the law on occasion, in a variety of ways, giving rise to under-standable claims of selective or inconsistent application of the law. The controversy that became public in May of 2013 surrounding the IRS's admittedly improper handling of certain nonprofit organizations based on their political views serves only to fuel perceptions of selective and inconsistent enforcement.

Given the untenable mix of vagueness in the law, violations without consequences, limited and inconsistent enforcement, and the lack of respect for the law and its administration that inevitably results, something needs to change.

A key principle on which there is much accord among the members of the Commission and its Panels is the idea that a member of the clergy should be permitted to say whatever he or she believes is appropriate in the context of a religious worship service without fear of government reprisal, even when such communications include content related to political candidates. At the same time, there is a high level of agreement among Commission and Panel members that permitting the disbursement of funds by tax-exempt religious and other 501(c)(3) organizations for political campaign activities could have a deleterious impact on the

(L to R) John Van Drunen, Michael E. Batts, Dan Busby, Michael Martin

effectiveness of the nonprofit sector. The Commission
. . . recommendations strike a necessary balance of
permitting religious and other nonprofit organizations
to engage in communications that are relevant to their
exempt purposes while ensuring that such organizations expend their funds in a manner consistent with
their tax-exempt charitable, religious, educational, and
similar purposes.

Post-Commission Era

The two Commission reports present thoughtful recommendations to resolve some of the most significant tax,
accountability, and policy issues facing churches and other
nonprofit organizations today. (Both reports are available at
ReligiousPolicyCommission.org.)

The question often arises: What was the impact of the two
reports prepared by the Commission and will the impact
continue into the future? Consider each of the reports:

1. The first report: *Enhancing Accountability for the
    Religious and Broader Nonprofit Sector.* While Senator
    Grassley's staff was desirous to see the Commission
    recommend additional legislation impacting churches
    and other nonprofit organizations, after careful
    consideration and thoughtful deliberation, the
    Commission recommended against additional
    legislation, except in one minor area.

    To date, additional legislation has not been adopted
    regarding any of the topics studied by the Commission.

Plus, the Commission's extensive research and documentation on the issues studied has been helpful in addressing these important topics.

2. The second report: *Government Regulation of Political Speech by Religious and Other 501(c)(3) Organizations: Why the Status Quo Is Untenable and Proposed Solutions.* This issue did not relate to the initial investigation of the six ministries by Senator Grassley. The senator added the issue to the list for consideration by the Commission because of his deep interest in the topic.

    The status quo in this area is increasingly untenable as legal pressure is brought on the IRS to enforce the political speech law that some believe is unconstitutional. At the same time, there are no indications that the IRS is enforcing the law. And, in each election cycle, more and more clergy are speaking their conscience on candidates and social issues, in defiance of the law.

    This crescendo is building to a climax that may lead to a much-needed change in the law. If the Commission's recommendation, or something similar, is adopted by Congress, it would result in the greatest protection of religious speech for leaders of all faiths that we have experienced since 1954.

Only time will tell how the Lord might use the Commission's work to make a lasting impact on the religious and broader nonprofit sector.

Chapter Eight

The Next Frontiers

> "The story of ECFA is best understood
> looking back over its formative years with thanksgiving
> for God's faithfulness to us. But ECFA's future
> must be lived out looking forward *and* upward."
>
> Dan Busby

*"Sow your seed in the morning, and at evening let your hands
not be idle, for you do not know which will succeed, whether
this or that, or whether both will do equally well."*
Ecclesiastes 11:6 (NIV)

All along, ECFA's posture has been to work faithfully and
tirelessly in the fields God sets before us following this
counsel of King Solomon. This describes board members,
senior leaders, and staff throughout ECFA's history. But what
does the future hold?

"Trying to predict the future is like trying to drive down a
country road at night with no lights while looking out the
back window," said Peter Drucker.

Even with several decades of solid history in the books, it is impossible to fully measure the impact ECFA has had in the past and that it will continue to have in the future. We have sown seeds in many fields consistent with our mission, and the first fruits we are reaping give us hope in at least four areas worth noting:

1. Impacting Christian Thought

While ECFA has been viewed throughout the years as a leader in providing information on "compliance" linked to financial and tax issues, with the publishing of a new series of books starting in 2010 under the name ECFAPress, ECFA is developing a reputation as a "thought leader" in the Christ-centered community.

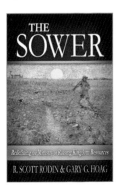

In 2010, Scott Rodin and Gary Hoag authored the first ECFAPress volume, *The Sower: Redefining the Ministry of Raising Kingdom Resources*. This book helped leaders integrate their faith and fundraising on both the theological and practical levels. It is viewed by many as the fundraising standard for Christ-centered ministries.

Later in 2010 from ECFAPress, David McKenna authored *Stewards of a Sacred Trust*. This volume covered the topics of CEO selection, transition, and development for boards of Christ-centered organizations.

In 2014, Gary Hoag, Scott Rodin, and Wesley Willmer authored another ECFAPress book, *The Choice: The Christ-Centered Pursuit of Kingdom Outcomes.*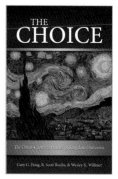
For Christ-followers serving in a society that values people and measures success based on metrics and results, this book offers a Christ-centered pathway that helps God's people focus on faithfulness, which is the only path that leads to ministry fruitfulness. It also helps Christ-followers navigate deep questions, such as "How do we define and measure success in ministry?" Endorsed widely by ministry leaders, *The Choice* is significantly influencing Christian thought.

In 2015, Dan Busby wrote the ECFAPress book, *TRUST: The Firm Foundation for Kingdom Fruitfulness.* This book is a comprehensive manual for building and maintaining trust in ministry today. It is filled with wit and wisdom for navigating the issues that swirl around governance, financial management, and raising resources. The key theme Dan communicates throughout the book is "Trust changes everything."

2. International Accountability Impact

For many years, ECFA has freely shared its knowledge about peer accountability with Christian leaders from around the world. Individuals from various countries have traveled to

ECFA's office at their own expense to learn more about our accreditation principles. Many have translated the ECFA standards into their native languages.

ECFA does not develop its own operational centers outside of the United States, because we cannot review compliance with regulations in other nations and cultural settings. However, ECFA is committed to encouraging and sharing accreditation concepts with leaders planning to develop such entities from around the world.

For example, in 2010, Pastor Sam Ko, a senior staff member at SaRang Church, Seoul, South Korea, met with Dan Busby, ECFA's president, at Washington Dulles International Airport. Sam expressed interest in SaRang Church becoming ECFA-accredited. As ECFA does not accredit internationally-based churches or ministries, a friendship developed and the initial conversation led to a series of additional meetings with SaRang Church leaders.

Sam Ko
Director of Global
Ministries
SaRang Church
Seoul, South Korea

In May 2014, Pastor Sam Ko and Ho Chan Hwang, the dean of the college and graduate school of business administration at Sejong University, asked if they could come to the ECFA offices to learn more about the history of the ECFA as a basis for forming a similar organization in South Korea. Dr. Hwang had studied in the U.S. many years ago and has been praying for a financial transparency organization to be formed in his home country for nearly three decades, ever since he received a copy of the 1987 edition of *Accounting and Financial Reporting Guide for Christian Ministries*.

ECFA asked Gary Hoag to moderate meetings between ECFA leaders and South Korean leaders. Dr. Hoag was chosen because of his extensive knowledge of the Korean culture and relationships formed on numerous international ministry trips.

Gary Hoag
ECFA International
Liaison (2014–Present)

After fruitful meetings, Dr. Hoag was appointed to serve on a part-time basis as the ECFA International Liaison. His role would be to work alongside Dan Busby and John Van Drunen to build a global network of leaders committed to the faithful administration of God's work. An unanticipated blessing from this work has been that these international leaders have expressed an interest in helping ECFA better serve the wide array of ethnically-diverse ministries in America that are not presently among the ranks of its membership.

In October 2014, John Van Drunen and Gary Hoag traveled to South Korea, representing ECFA at the invitation of SaRang Church. The purpose of this trip was five-fold: (1) to sign a Memorandum of Understanding between ECFA and the new Korean peer accountability organization, Christian Council for Financial Transparency, Korea (CCFK), (2) to discuss financial accountability with Korean Church leaders, (3) to explore transparency issues with parachurch leaders, (4) to build

awareness and membership of CCFK through the media, and
(5) to foster key relationships. The trip far exceeded expectations thanks to the hand of God and assistance from ECFA
Korean Advisor, Dr. Sung Wook Chung.

(L to R) Ho Chan Hwang, Gary Hoag, Jung Hyun Oh (senior pastor of
SaRang Church, Seoul, South Korea), John Van Drunen
(during October 2014 trip)

CCFK achieved official government status in December 2014,
with 2015 as a season for founding members to join. On June
27, 2015, Dr. Hoag and Dr. Chung attended the formal
celebration of the launching of CCFK with twenty members:
ten churches and ten parachurch ministries.

The fruitful interaction with Korean leaders was a key factor
in ECFA convening the first-ever International Accountability
Summit (IAS) on April 14, 2015 in Dallas, TX facilitated by
Gary Hoag. The aim of that event was four-fold: (1) to develop
a community of representatives, (2) to set a framework for
collaboration, (3) to form a global support network, and

(4) to discuss international standards. Attendees represented the following nations: Australia, Ecuador, Guatemala, Hong Kong and China, India, Kenya, Philippines, South Korea, United Kingdom, Ukraine, Uruguay, and the USA.

Attendees at the International Accountability Summit, April 13-14, 2015, Dallas, TX

After the IAS event, it was evident to all who attended that God is raising up capable and committed leaders around the world who desire to form peer accountability organizations. To serve this global community of leaders, a quarterly newsletter, the Global Network Update, and a webpage on the ECFA website, were created to archive the content of the IAS, to provide a platform for the global sharing of resources, and to unite international leaders in faithful prayer.

On September 19–22, 2015, Ho Chan Hwang and Sam Ko returned the favor ECFA had extended to them. They traveled to America and passionately encouraged a group of Korean-American church and ministry leaders convened by Sung Wook Chung to join ECFA. ECFA is already beginning to see a growing interest from Korean-American churches and ministries as a result of the gathering.

On October 7–13, 2015, in response to an invitation from Mr. Angelito Gabriel and Dr. Zenet Maramara at the IAS event, Drs. Gary Hoag and Wes Willmer travelled to Manila, Philippines, with three aims: (1) to build relationships with these key national leaders, (2) to catalyze the CCTA Board (the Christian Council for Transparency and Accountability had been formed as an organization three years earlier but was not operating), and (3) to provide trainings for church and ministry leaders on the faithful administration and governance of God's work. These aims and more were accomplished thanks to prayer from the global network of leaders around the world and the blessing of God.

Looking ahead, in 2015, Dr. Gary Hoag anticipates visits to IAS attendees in four to six countries. Our international collaboration seeks to ultimately strengthen the believers in these nations, so that we can strengthen the churches and ministries they serve for God's glory.

3. Church Initiative

When ECFA was formed in 1979, there was no intention of excluding churches from accreditation. In fact, church leaders participated in the founding meetings.

However, the specific wording of some ECFA standards related more to parachurch ministries than to churches. For example, the term "fundraising" was used—a term more closely identified with parachurch ministries. The parallel term for churches is "stewardship." While some churches like Willow Creek Community Church, South Barrington, Illinois, were early adopters of ECFA accreditation, relatively few churches became members in the first three decades of ECFA's history.

In 2009, ECFA began to explore ways to reach out to churches that may qualify for membership. Between 2009 and 2015, these early steps included:

- Identifying churches with attendance around 750 or more as being most likely to meet ECFA's standards,

- Modifications to the ECFA mission statement, standards and commentaries, making them more relevant for churches,

- Distinguishing documents in the online Knowledge Center between church and parachurch documents,

- Offering church-specific webinars and videos,

- Conducting church-specific stewardship, financial management, and governance surveys, and

- Developing a special website just for churches.

Presently, ECFA's membership includes churches from more than 18 different denominations and over 30 of the largest and fastest-growing congregations in the United States. ECFA's church membership and outreach to all churches will be elevated with the formal launch of the church initiative in 2016.

In 2015, ECFA was awarded a grant from the Lilly Endowment of Indianapolis to strengthen ECFA's capacity to provide financial literacy resources to churches and clergy. The three-year grant (2016–2018) will help ECFA expand its outreaches to churches in the years ahead.

4. ECFA's Impact Beyond Its Members

Recognizing that tens of thousands of smaller churches and ministries may never meet all of ECFA's standards necessary to become accredited, in 2011, ECFA began to offer certain educational materials at no or minimal cost to non-member organizations. These offerings included:

- Monthly electronic newsletters: the *ChurchPulse* was widely circulated to churches, and the *NonprofitPulse* was distributed to nonprofit ministries,

- ChurchWise.org and NonprofitWise.org,

- Videos and webinars, and

- Workshops at national conferences.

These outreaches to all organizations in the body of Christ are critical to ECFA fulfilling its mission.

Looking Forward and Upward

In the years to come, ECFA will continue to focus faithfully on its mission, "Enhancing Trust in Christ-Centered Churches and Ministries." ECFA's first commitment must always be to its accredited members, followed by its desire to impact non-accredited Christ-centered churches and ministries in America and internationally. We rejoice that groups around the world seek to join us in this global work and even assist us with our domestic efforts.

Even at the 37-year point, it is impossible to fully measure the impact ECFA has had in the past and that it will have in the future.

Appendix 1

The Seven Standards of Responsible Stewardship—2016

STANDARD 1

Doctrinal Issues – Every organization shall subscribe to a written statement of faith clearly affirming a commitment to the evangelical Christian faith or shall otherwise demonstrate such commitment, and shall operate in accordance with biblical truths and practices.

STANDARD 2

Governance – Every organization shall be governed by a responsible board of not less than five individuals, a majority of whom shall be independent, who shall meet at least semiannually to establish policy and review its accomplishments.

STANDARD 3

Financial Oversight – Each organization shall prepare complete and accurate financial statements. The board or a committee consisting of a majority of independent members shall approve the engagement of an independent certified public accountant, review the annual financial statements and maintain appropriate communication with the independent certified public accountant.

The board shall be apprised of any material weaknesses in internal control or other significant risks.

STANDARD **4**

Use of Resources and Compliance with Laws – Every organization shall exercise the appropriate management and controls necessary to provide reasonable assurance that all of the organization's operations are carried out and resources are used in a responsible manner and in conformity with applicable laws and regulations, such conformity taking into account biblical mandates.

STANDARD **5**

Transparency – Every organization shall provide a copy of its current financial statements upon written request and shall provide other disclosures as the law may require. The financial statements required to comply with Standard 3 must be disclosed under this standard.

An organization must provide a report, upon written request, including financial information on any specific project for which it has sought or is seeking gifts.

STANDARD **6**

Compensation-Setting and Related-Party Trans-actions – Every organization shall set compensation of its top leader and address related-party transactions in a manner that demonstrates integrity and propriety in conformity with ECFA's Policy for Excellence in Compensation-Setting and Related-Party Transactions.

STANDARD 7
Stewardship of Charitable Gifts

7.1 Truthfulness in Communications – In securing charitable gifts, all representations of fact, descriptions of the financial condition of the organization, or narratives about events must be current, complete, and accurate. References to past activities or events must be appropriately dated. There must be no material omissions or exaggerations of fact, use of misleading photographs or any other communication which would tend to create a false impression or misunderstanding.

7.2 Giver Expectations and Intent – Statements made about the use of gifts by an organization in its charitable gift appeals must be honored. A giver's intent relates both to what was communicated in the appeal and to any instructions accompanying the gift, if accepted by the organization. Appeals for charitable gifts must not create unrealistic expectations of what a gift will actually accomplish.

7.3 Charitable Gift Communication – Every organization shall provide givers appropriate and timely gift acknowledgments.

7.4 Acting in the Best Interest of Givers – When dealing with persons regarding commitments on major gifts, an organization's representatives must seek to guide and advise givers to adequately consider their broad interests.

An organization must make every effort to avoid knowingly accepting a gift from, or entering into a contract with, a giver that would place a hardship on the giver or place the giver's future well-being in jeopardy.

7.5 Percentage Compensation for Securing Charitable Gifts – An organization may not base compensation of outside stewardship resource consultants or its own employees directly or indirectly on a percentage of charitable contributions raised.

Appendix 2

ECFA's Initial Standards—1981

Standard 1—Every member organization shall subscribe to a written statement of faith clearly affirming its commitment to the evangelical Christian faith.

Standard 2—Every member organization shall be governed by a responsible board, the majority of whose members shall not be employees/staff, and/or related by blood or marriage to such, which shall meet at least semi-annually to establish policy and review its accomplishment.

Standard 3—Every member organization shall obtain an annual audit performed by an independent public accounting firm in accordance with generally accepted auditing standards (GAAS) with financial statements prepared in accordance with generally accepted accounting principles (GAAP).

Standard 4—Every member organization shall have a functioning audit review committee appointed by the board, a majority of whom shall not be employees/staff and/or related by blood or marriage, for the purpose of reviewing the annual audit and reporting its findings to the board.

Standard 5—Every member organization shall provide a copy of its current audited financial statements upon written request.

Standard 6—Every member organization should conduct its activities with the highest standards of integrity and avoid conflicts of interest.

Standard 7—Every member organization shall ensure that its fund-raising appeals clearly identify the purposes and programs to which the donations shall be applied and shall ensure that these donations are used for the purpose to which they were raised.

Appendix 3

ECFA's Fundraising Standards Added in 1987

1. **Truthfulness in Communication:** All representations of fact, description of financial condition of the organization, or narrative about events must be current, complete and accurate. References to past activities or events must be appropriately dated. There must be no material omissions or exaggerations of fact or use of misleading photographs or any other communication which would tend to create a false impression or misunderstanding.

2. **Communications and Donor Expectations:** Fundraising appeals must not create unrealistic donor expectations of what a donor's gift will actually accomplish within the limits of the organization's ministry.

3. **Communication and Donor Intent:** All statements made by the organization in its fundraising appeals about the use of the gift must be honored by the organization. The donor's intent is related to both what was communication in the appeal and to any donor instructions accompanying the gift. The organization should be aware that communications made in

fundraising appeals may create a legally binding restriction.

4. **Projects Unrelated to a Ministry's Primary Purpose:** An organization raising or receiving funds for programs that are not part of its present or prospective ministry, but are proper in accordance with its exempt purpose, must either treat them as restricted funds and channel them through an organization that can carry out the donor's intent, or return the funds to the donor.

5. **Incentives and Premiums:** Fundraising appeals which offer premiums or incentives, the value of which is not insubstantial, but which is significant in relation to the amount of the donation, must advise the donor, both in the solicitation and in the receipt, of the fair market value of the premium or incentive and that the value is not deductible for tax purposes.

6. **Reporting:** An organization must provide, on request, a report, including financial information on the project for which it is soliciting gifts.

7. **Percentage Compensation for Fundraisers:** Compensation of outside fundraising consultants based directly or indirectly on a percentage of what is raised, or on any other contingency agreement, may create potential conflicts and opportunities for abuse. Full disclosure of such arrangements is required, at least annually, in the organization's audited financial statements, in which the disclosure must match income and

related expenses. Compensation to the organization's own employees on a percentage basis or contingency basis is not allowed.

8. **Tax Deductible Gifts for a Named Recipient's Personal Benefit:** Tax deductible gifts may not be used to pass money or benefits to any named individual for personal use.

9. **Conflict of Interest on Royalties:** An officer, director, or other principal of the organization must not receive royalties for any product that is used for fundraising or promotional purposes by his/her own organization.

10. **Acknowledgement of Gifts in Kind:** Property or gifts in kind received by an organization should be acknowledged describing the property or gift accurately without a statement of the gift's market value. It is the responsibility of the donor to determine the fair market value of the property for tax purposes.

11. **Acting in the Interest of the Donor:** An organization must make every effort to avoid accepting a gift from or entering into a contract with a prospective donor which would knowingly place a hardship on the donor, or place the donor's future well-being in jeopardy.

12. **Financial advice:** The representative of the organization, when dealing with persons regarding commitments on major estate assets, must seek to guide and

advise donors so they have adequately considered the broad interests of the family and the various ministries they are currently supporting before they make a final decision. Donors should be encouraged to use the services of their attorneys, accountants, or other professional advisors.

Appendix 4

Compensation-Setting Provisions Added to Standard 6 Effective January 1, 2014

Effective January 1, 2014, ECFA revised Standard 6, taking compensation-setting practices to a higher level, by adding new policies for setting compensation for top leaders of its member organizations. Revisions were also made to guidelines on related-party transactions to ensure utmost integrity in all agreements.

Standard 6 was revised to read: "Every organization shall set compensation of its top leader and address related-party transactions in a manner that demonstrates integrity and propriety in conformity with ECFA's Policy for Excellence in Compensation-Setting and Related-Party Transactions."

Under the revised standard, member ministries with higher paid leaders are required to perform minimum due diligence to ensure reasonable total compensation, while all organizations are encouraged to adopt the practices. Related-party transactions must be conducted in a manner that demonstrates integrity and propriety according to ECFA's high standards. Specific guidelines are detailed in ECFA's Policy for Excellence in Compensation-Setting and Related-Party Transactions.

Appendix 5

ECFA's First Financial Disclosure Committee, Board of Directors, and Standards Committee

ECFA's Financial Disclosure Committee – June 12, 1978

Aarsvold, Joel, Billy Graham Evangelistic Association

Canning, James, Ernst & Ernst

Engstrom, Ted (Chairman), World Vision

Gustavson, Brandt, Moody Bible Institute

Howard, Eldon J., Sudan Interior Mission

Jones, Melvin, Back to the Bible

ECFA's First Board of Directors – September 11, 1979

Aarsvold, Joel (Secretary), Billy Graham Evangelistic Association

Bridges, Jerry (Standards Committee Chairman), The Navigators

Capin, Richard (Treasurer), CapinCrouse

Engstrom, Ted (Chairman), World Vision

Gustavson, Brandt (Vice Chairman), Moody Bible Institute

Howard, Eldon J., Sudan Interior Mission

Long, Stanley, Tom Skinner Associates

Loux, Gordon, Prison Fellowship

Mooneyham, Stanley, World Vision

Olson, Lloyd, Campus Crusade for Christ

Wilson, George, Billy Graham Evangelistic Association

ECFA's First Standards Committee – June 26, 1979

Bergstedt, Alan, World Vision

Bridges, Jerry (Chairman), The Navigators

Canning, James, Ernst & Ernst

Glavich, Victor, Youth for Christ International

Grange, George, Gammon & Grange

Hales, Edward, First Baptist Church, Portland, ME

Mortenson, Donald, Seattle Pacific University

Appendix 6

ECFA's Board Members

Board Member	Terms	Offices Held
Aarsvold, Joel B.	79-84; 87-93	Secretary 79-81
Addington, Tom	00-06; 11-present	Treasurer 01 Chair 02-04
Alvis, Rick	12-present	Treasurer 13-16
Antrim, Barbara	91-96	
Augsburger, Myron	91-96	
Basinger, Rebekah	01-07	Secretary 05-06
Batts, Michael	05-14; 15-present	Treasurer 06 Chair 07-09 Vice Chair 15-16
Beckman, Marvin	88-92	
Bennett, John	85-86	
Bettencourt, Sam	06-09	
Boone, Wellington	95-99	
Bourke, Dale H.	05-07	
Bridges, Jerry	79-87; 88-94	Chair SC, 79-86 Vice Chair 89-90 Chair 91

Brown, John	85-93; 03-09	Secretary 87, 04 Vice Chair 88 Chair 89-90; 05-06
Burger, Stephen E.	87-93	
Busby, Dan	04	
Capin, Richard F.	79-85; 86-92	Treasurer 79-83; 89-91 Vice Chair 84 Chair 85
Cerutti, Frank L.	89-95; 97-00	Treasurer 92-94
Cole, Erika	13-present	
Cook, Clyde	81-82	
de Armas, Danny	14-present	
Delahoyde, Melinda	10-13; 13-16	
Delcamp, Samuel L.	85-91	
DeMoss, Ted	82-85	
Dingman, Robert	99-04	Vice Chair 00
Douglass, Stephen B.	86-92	
Doyle, Christopher	02-08	
Engstrom, Ted W.	79-94	Chair 79-81
Entwistle, Lorrance	91-93	
Ericksen, Donald O.	85-87	
Godwin, Joyce	96-02	Chair 99-01
Grange, George R.	80-86; 87-88	Secretary 82-84 Vice Chair 85 Chair 86
Gustavson, Brandt	79-84; 88-94; 96-01	Vice Chair 79-81 Secretary 99-00

Hales, Edward J.	84-87	
Hammar, Richard	96-02	
Hescott, Donald E.	85-88	
Holbrook, Mark	07-13	Secretary 08 Vice Chair 09 Chair 10-12
Howard, Eldon J.	79-80; 82-88	Treasurer 86-87
Humphries, Cary	94-00	Chair 97-98
Johnston, David E.	82-86	Treasurer 84-85
Kesler, Jay	85-88	
Kliewer, Bill	86-88	
Larkin, Richard F.	86-92	
Larson, Kenneth	95-01; 02-08; 11-present	Treasurer 98-00; 02-03 Vice Chair 04-07 Secretary 13-16
Libby, Lauren	98-04; 05-14	Secretary 01-03 Treasurer 09-12
Little, Michael	98-04; 05-10; 11-present	Secretary 09 Vice Chair 13-14 Chair 15-16
Long, Stanley B.	79-85; 86	
Loritts, Crawford	98-04	
Lotz, Anne Graham	98-02	
Loux, Gordon D.	79-85; 86-92	Vice Chair 82-83; 86 Chair 87-88
Lyon, Jo Anne	08-14	
Magnuson, Warren R.	85-92	Treasurer 88
Martin, Cheryl	10-15	

McCabe, Tom	92-98; 01-04	Chair 92-94 Treasurer 96-97
McCallie, Thomas	03-08	
Moody, George	94-97	Vice Chair 95-96
Mooneyham, Stanley	79-82	
Morehead, Jean	91-97	
Morgan, Elisa	03-09	Treasurer 07-08
Mortenson, Don	94-97	
Mulder, Dennis M.	89-95	Secretary 93 Vice Chair 94
Nash, Sylvia D.	83-89	
Nelson, Paul	91-93	Vice Chair 92-93
Olson, Lloyd	79-85	
Patterson, Virginia	84-90; 95-01	Secretary 85-86; 95-98
Peabody, Snow	89-94	Vice Chair 91
Pearson, John W.	89-95	Secretary 91-92
Pederson, Wayne	10-16	
Peek, Warren	14-present	
Rainey, Dennis	97-00	
Reid, Russ	87-90	
Reimer, Clarence	84-87; Emeritus	Vice Chair 87
Rhoads, Ross S.	85-92	Secretary 88-90
Robertson, Dwight	12-present	
Rogers, George W.	80-83	
Sindorf, Kathy	09-15	Secretary 10-12
Smith, Efrem	15-present	

Sparks, Carolyn	02-05	
Stearns, Richard	00-06	Treasurer 04-05
Swonger, Donald E.	80	
Thomann, Randy	08-11	
Van Broekhoven, Rollin	87-93; 94-00; 01-04	Secretary 94 Chair 95-96 Vice Chair 97-99; 01-03
Weary, Dolphus	92-96; 97-03; 04-10	
White, Jerry	13-present	
Wiebe, Virgil	92-96	Treasurer 95
Wills, David	09-15	Vice Chair 10-12 Chair 13-14
Willmer, Wesley	04-09	Secretary 07 Vice Chair 08
Wilson, George M.	79-85; 86-92; 93-94; Emeritus	Chair 82-84
Wright, Frank	08-11	
Wynn, Richard R.	90-91	
Yasuda, John	06-12	
Zimmerman, Thomas	85-86	

Appendix 7

ECFA's Standards Committee Members

Committee Member	Terms	Offices Held
Altman, Bill	85-99	
Alvis, Rick	00-05	
Anderson, Ed	95-00; 07-12	
Anderson, Robert	94-96	
Batts, Michael	02-06; 11-12	Chair 11-12
Bergstedt, Alan	79-84	Secretary 79-84
Bridges, Jerry	79-86	Chair 79-86
Busby, Dan	90-95; 97-99; 04	Chair 04 Acting Secretary 05-07
Canning, James	79-84	
Capin, Gregg	87-98; 01-06	
Carey, Amy Bragg	07-12	
Casey, Kenneth R.	86-93	
Cerutti, Frank L.	95-99	Secretary 96 Chairman 97-99
Cocanower, Harold	87-90	
Coleman, David	07-09	
Davis, Mark	07-12	

Durman, Barry	97-99	Secretary 99
Dixon, Larry	81-85	
Edwards, Norman	81-85; 92-94	
Ely, Fred	93-98; 02-07	Secretary 97-98
Falin, John	04-07	
Glavach, Victor	79-86	
Grange, George	79-81	
Hales, Edward	79-86; 91-96	
Haupt, Major Gary	09-10	
Hazelton, Dean	81-82	
Holbrook, Scott	06-12	
James, Julie	07-12	
Koltveit, Jim	99-01	
Karppinen, Richard	87-91; 93-98	
Klingbeil, Tim	98-03	Secretary 00-03
Lawson, David	98-03	
Libby, Lauren	05-07	Chair 05-07
Lyon, Jo Anne	05-07	
Martin, Robert	87-90	Secretary 87
Mason, Richard	88-93	
McCabe, Thomas	86-92; 00-03	Chair 01-03
McFarland, Steve	95-97	
Mortenson, Donald	79-85; 87-96	Secretary 89-93 Chair 94, 95, 96
Nicholaou, Nick	97-02	

Owens, Greg	07-12	
Plunkett, Shari	91-96; 99-04	
Repass, Cindi	05-10	
Roys, Susan	95-97	
Russ, Douglass	85-88	
Smith, Max	96-01	
Steinhagen, Robert	04-09	
Thomann, Randy	96-01; 03-10	Chair 08-10
Van Broekhoven, Rollin	82-93; 00	Chair 87-93; 00
Vander Kooi, Sandi	99-04	
Vinkemulder, Yvonne	90-95	Secretary 94-95
Wallace, Nicholas	07-12	
Wilhem, Carl	83-86	

Appendix 8

ECFA's Standards Advisory Committee

Member	Years of Service
Barr, James R.	2013-Present
Capin, Gregg	2013-Present
Hadley, Kimberly M.	2013-Present
Kemp, Dale Allen	2013-Present
King, Donald	2013-Present
Kraske, Scott	2013-Present
Linch, Cathi M.	2013-2015
Littlejohn, C. Merrill	2013-Present
Neal, Jennifer	2013-Present
Newberg, Brian	2013-Present
Trusty, Delanie	2013-Present

Appendix 9

Evolution of the ECFA
Member Seal and Logo

1979

1981

1981

Tenth Anniversary
Logo – 1989

Twentieth Anniversary
Logo – 1999

The symbol of trust

2000

A higher standard.
A higher purpose.

2003

A higher standard.
A higher purpose.

2003

Enhancing Trust

2012

Enhancing Trust

2012

Endnotes

Introduction

[1] Carl Bakal, "Where Do Charity Billions Go?" *Parade*, January 6, 1980, 21–22.

[2] James A. Canning, "Financial Accountability in Nonprofit Organizations: The Impact of the Evangelical Council for Financial Accountability (ECFA)" (doctoral thesis, Claremont Graduate Univ., 2002), 171–72.

Chapter One – Before There Was an ECFA

[1] National Association of Evangelicals, "What is an Evangelical?," http://nae.net/what-is-an-evangelical/.

[2] Alexis De Tocqueville, *Democracy in America*, ed. Harvey C. Mansfield and Delba Winthrop (Univ. of Chicago, 2000), 489.

[3] Brice S. McKeever, "The Nonprofit Sector in Brief 2015: Public Charities, Giving, and Volunteering," The Urban Institute, October 2015, 2.

[4] Cheryl Chasin, Debra Kawecki and David Jones, "Form 990," *IRS Exempt Organization Continuing Professional Education Text* (2002), 227–28.

[5] ECFA interview with Stephen Douglass, August 3, 2011.

[6] Bakal, "Where Do Charity Billions Go?" 21–22.

[7] Ibid., 22.

[8] Donald P. Baker, "Secrecy Veils Pallottine Fathers' Mail Order Colossus," *The Pittsburgh Press*, December 14, 1975.

Chapter Two – Peer Accountability Takes Hold

[1] Martin Luther King, Jr., "MLK Quote of the Week: Faith is taking the First Step...," The King Center, February 21, 2013, http://www.thekingcenter.org/blog/mlk-quote-week-faith-taking-first-step.

[2] Eldon Howard served as the USA Treasurer before becoming International Treasurer, then Chief Financial Officer, and finally Deputy General Director of SIM, Charlotte, NC—an ECFA charter member. Eldon chaired the Interdenominational Foreign Missions Association (IFMA) Accounting Task Force that produced the *Accounting and Financial Reporting Guide for Christian Ministries* published jointly by IFMA, Evangelical Foreign Missions Association (EFMA), Christian Ministries Management Association (CMMA), and ECFA in December 1987.

[3] John Maust, "Voluntary Disclosure: So Far So Credible," *Christianity Today*, October 5, 1979, 57–58.

[4] ECFA Interview with Chip Grange, July 19, 2011.

[5] Ibid.

Chapter Three – Blazing the Trail

[1] Art Borden testimony before the U.S. Senate Finance Committee, September 30, 1983.

[2] Gordon Loux testimony before the U.S. House Ways and Means Committee, October 6, 1987.

[3] The cash basis of accounting only reflects cash received and disbursed, with no reflection of receivables, payables, or capitalized assets. The modified accrual basis of accounting recognizes revenues when they become available and measurable and, with a few exceptions, recognizes expenditures when liabilities are incurred.

[4] J. Michael Martin, "Nonprofits Need Standards Too: The Development of U.S Financial Accounting and Reporting Standards

for Nonprofit Organizations Over the Last Forty Years," (research paper, Liberty Univ., 2014), 8–9.

[5] Gary L.Tidwell, "Was Maintaining the Executive Payroll at PTL an Example of Auditor Independence?" in W. Michael Hoffman, et al., *The Ethics of Accounting & Finance: Trust, Responsibility, and Control* (Westport, CT: Greenwood Publishing, 1996), 102–3.

[6] Ibid., 108.

[7] Ibid.

[8] Ibid.

[9] Mark Ward, Sr., *Air of Salvation* (Grand Rapids, Mich.: Baker Books, 1994), 172–74.

[10] Ibid., 177–79.

[11] Ibid., 222.

[12] ECFA interview with Tom McCabe, February 26, 2011.

Chapter Four – Facing Challenges

[1] Gilbert M. Gaul, "Panel Will Act To Curb Abuses By Nonprofits Under a House Sub-Committee Plan, The IRS Could Fine Groups That Use Funds To Enrich Officers And Directors," *The Philadelphia Inquirer*, December 11, 1993, http://articles.philly.com/1993-12-11/news/25941222_1_tax-exempt-organizations-irs-abuses.

[2] Niles C. Logue, "The 'Dogged' College Professor vs. The 'King' of Charitable Giving: A Lesson in Professional Stewardship from The Foundation for New Era Philanthropy" (Messiah College, 2000), 111.

[3] Ibid., 114.

[4] Ibid., 134.

[5] Ibid., 135.

[6] Ibid., 116–17.

[7] Ibid., 134.

[8] Ibid., 114.

[9] Ibid., 123.

[9] "Head of Bankrupt Charity Fund Pleads No Contest in Fraud Case," *The New York Times*, March 27, 1997: www.nytimes.com/1997/03/27/business/head-of-bankrupt-charity-fund-pleads-no-contest-in-fraud-case.html.

[10] Tony Casnes, "Bennett Confesses 'Dream' Became 'Delusion,'" *Christianity Today*, October 27, 1997, 90.

Chapter Five – Expanding Impact

[1] Todd Starnes, "Arizona Baptist Foundation Announces Liquidation Plans," *Baptist Press*, December 17, 1999, http://www.bpnews.net/4393/arizona-baptist-foundation-announces-liquidation-plans.

[2] Terry Pristin and Nina Bernstein, "Ex-Head of Hale House and Husband Charged With Theft," *New York Times*, February 6, 2002, http://www.nytimes.com/2002/02/06/nyregion/ex-head-of-hale-house-and-husband-charged-with-theft.html.

[3] Chuck Fager, "Fraud: Greater Ministries Leaders Get Lengthy Prison Terms," *Christianity Today*, October 1, 2001, http://www.christianitytoday.com/ct/2001/october1/15.21.html.

[4] Wesley Willmer, *Revolution in Generosity* (Chicago, IL: Moody Publishers, 2008), 401. The Biblical Principles for Stewardship and Fundraising are available at ECFA.org/Content/Biblical-Principles-for-Stewardship-and-Fundraising.

[5] Independent Sector (independentsector.org) is a Washington, D.C.-based organization whose mission is to advance the common good by leading, strengthening, and mobilizing the nonprofit and philanthropic community.

⁶ The annual *audit* by an independent CPA firm—required for larger ECFA member organizations—helps ensure, and is evidence of, financial accountability to an organization's constituencies. The independent auditor tests the data underlying the financial statements to form an opinion on the fairness of their presentation in accordance with U.S. generally accepted accounting principles (GAAP). The auditor's standard report provides reasonable assurance that the financial statements are free of material misstatements. Knowing they can rely on the accuracy of the organization's financial statements, the board and management can make wise and perceptive policy decisions. *Note:* Obtaining an audit may be required to comply with state law.

An annual *review* by an independent CPA firm is permitted for ECFA member organizations of medium revenue size and provides limited assurance of the reasonableness of the financial statements presented. Although not as comprehensive as an audit, a review provides more assurance on the financial statements than a compilation. A review report states that: 1) the accountants do not express an opinion on the financial statements, and 2) based on their review, they are not aware of any material modifications that should be made to the financial statements.

The annual *compilation* by an independent CPA firm, permitted for ECFA member organizations of smaller revenue size, is simply the gathering of financial information and the development of financial statements for an organization. (An otherwise independent CPA firm that performs outsourced accounting functions for the organization meets this requirement.) A compilation involves no assurance on the financial statements, as the accountant merely assembles the financial statements for the organization. The independent CPA's participation with the financial statements will often help stakeholders feel that the statements are prepared with knowledge of applicable standards.

For compilations and reviews to meet ECFA's requirements, the independent CPA must present the compiled or reviewed financial data according to GAAP or on the modified cash basis of accounting. If the modified cash basis of accounting is used, the financial statements must include the recognition of property and equipment as assets, depreciation as expense, and debt, other than trade payables and ordinary accruals, as liabilities.

Federal laws governing tax-exempt organizations generally do not require audits. However, many states, boards, and resource providers (such as donors, foundations, and financial institutions) see the involvement of an independent CPA firm as an essential and truly wise investment.

Chapter Seven – The Commission Era

[1] U.S. Senate Committee on Finance, "Grassley Seeks Information from Six Media-based Ministries," press release, November 6, 2007, http://www.finance.senate.gov/newsroom/ranking/release/?id=baa4251a-ee70-48af-a324-79801cd07f18.

[2] Senator Charles E. Grassley letter to ECFA President Dan Busby, January 5, 2011, religiouspolicycommission.org/Content/Grassley-letter-to-ECFA.

[3] Information regarding the Commission on Accountability and Policy for Religious Organizations is available at www.ReligiousPolicyCommission.org.

Members of the Commission and their affiliations at the time (2011–2013):

Mr. Michael E. Batts, Chairman, president and managing partner of Batts Morrison Wales & Lee, Orlando, FL

Mr. Dan Busby, president of ECFA, Winchester, VA

Rev. Luis Cortes, Jr., founder of Esperanza, Philadelphia, PA

Rev. Mark Davis, executive pastor of Calvary Chapel Fort Lauderdale, FL

Mr. Stephen Douglass, president of Cru, Orlando, FL

Mr. Richard Hammar, Attorney, CPA, general counsel for the Assemblies of God, Springfield, MO

Mr. Mark Holbrook, president and CEO of the Evangelical Christian Credit Union, Brea, CA

Dr. Joel Hunter, senior pastor of Northland, A Church Distributed, Longwood, FL

Mr. Lauren Libby, president of TWR, Cary, NC

Dr. Jo Anne Lyon, general superintendent of The Wesleyan Church, Indianapolis, IN

Rev. William Townes, Jr., vice president for convention finance for the Executive Committee of the Southern Baptist Convention, Nashville, TN

Dr. Kenneth Ulmer, senior pastor and teacher of Faithful Central Bible Church, Inglewood, CA

Dr. Dolphus Weary, president of the Rural Education and Leadership Christian Foundation, Richland, MI

Mr. David Wills, president of the National Christian Foundation, Alpharetta, GA

4 ECFA interview with Michael Batts, July 16, 2011.

Index

Why Do **Churches** Join **ECFA**?

To Demonstrate **Integrity!**

Life.Church's accreditation by ECFA serves as a clear statement of assurance to our attendees, our donors, and to the public that we conduct Kingdom business with integrity and accountability.

Craig Groeschel, Senior Pastor, Life.Church, Edmond, OK

Resources for Church Members

ChurchPulse Monthly eNewsletter

Educational Webinars and Videos

Knowledge Center Documents

Practical Policies for Church Use

Church Surveys with Latest Trends

Collaboration with Other Churches

Why Do **Ministries** Join **ECFA**?

To Demonstrate **Integrity!**

Compassion International is grateful to be a charter member of ECFA. We've found our accreditation to be immensely valuable in solidifying trust and integrity with donors throughout the evangelical community.

Santiago "Jimmy" Mellado, *President and CEO Compassion International, Colorado Springs, CO*

Resources for Nonprofit Members

NonprofitPulse
Monthly
eNewsletter

Educational
Webinars
and Videos

Knowledge
Center
Documents

Practical Policies
for Nonprofit Use

Nonprofit
Surveys with
Latest Trends

Compensation
Data Resource

For more information, visit **ECFA.org**

Resources Provided by ECFA and/or Authored by ECFA Staff

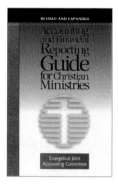

Accounting and Financial Reporting Guide for Christian Ministries
Evangelical Joint Accounting Committee — 2001

Donor-Restricted Gifts
Dan Busby — 2006

Donor-Restricted Gifts Simplified
Dan Busby — 2007

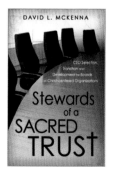

Stewards of a Sacred Trust
David McKenna — 2010

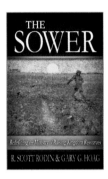

The Sower: Redefining the Ministry of Raising Kingdom Resources
Gary G. Hoag, R. Scott Rodin — 2010

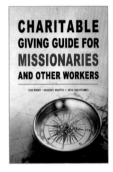

Charitable Giving Guide for Missionaries and Other Workers
Dan Busby, Michael Martin, John Van Drunen — 2013

Charitable Giving Guide for Short-Term Mission Trips
Dan Busby, Michael Martin, John Van Drunen — 2013

**The Choice: The Christ-Centered
Pursuit of Kingdom Outcomes**
Gary G. Hoag, R. Scott Rodin,
Wesley K. Willmer — 2014

**Trust: The Firm Foundation
for Kingdom Fruitfulness**
Dan Busby — 2015

**The Guide to Charitable Giving
for Churches and Ministries**
Dan Busby, Michael Martin,
John Van Drunen — 2015

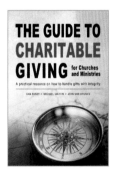

**Charitable Giving Guide
for Giver-Restricted Gifts**
Dan Busby, Michael Martin,
John Van Drunen — 2016

**Charitable Giving Guide
for Acknowledging and Reporting
Charitable Gifts**
Dan Busby, Michael Martin,
John Van Drunen — 2016

Church and Nonprofit Tax & Financial Guide
(published annually since 1992)
1992–2010
Dan Busby

2011–2012
Dan Busby, John Van Drunen

2013–Present
Dan Busby, Michael Martin,
John Van Drunen

Minister's Tax & Financial Guide
(published annually since 1992)
1992–2010
Dan Busby

2011–2012
Dan Busby, John Van Drunen

2013–Present
Dan Busby, Michael Martin,
John Van Drunen

Board Training Resources

Coming Soon

Series No. 4: Succession Planning

For more information on the resources shown in this section,
see **ECFA.org**.